C000097614

GLOBE...

Trave...

BUDAPEST
AND HUNGARY

BRIAN RICHARDS

NEW
HOLLAND

NEW
HOLLAND

*** Highly recommended
** Recommended
* See if you can

First edition published in 2002
by New Holland Publishers (UK) Ltd
London • Cape Town • Sydney • Auckland

10 9 8 7 6 5 4 3 2 1

website: www.newhollandpublishers.com

Garfield House, 86 Edgware Road
London W2 2EA
United Kingdom

80 McKenzie Street
Cape Town 8001
South Africa

14 Aquatic Drive
Frenchs Forest, NSW 2086
Australia

218 Lake Road
Northcote, Auckland
New Zealand

Distributed in the USA by
The Globe Pequot Press
Connecticut

Publishing Manager: John Loubser
Managing Editor: Thea Grobbelaar
DTP Cartographic Manager: Genené Hart
Editors: Melany McCallum, Thea Grobbelaar
Design and DTP: Lellyn Creamer
Cartographer: Nicole Engeler
Picture Researcher: Colleen Abrahams
Consultant: Steve Fallon
Indexer: Melany McCallum
Proofreader: Claudia Dos Santos

Reproduction by Hirt & Carter (Pty) Ltd, Cape Town
Printed and bound in Hong Kong by Sing Cheong
Printing Co. Ltd.

Photographic Credits:
Mark Azavedo Photo Library: pages 33, 57, 61;
Sylvia Cordaiy Photo Library/Gable: pages 36,
54, 119;
Sylvia Cordaiy Photo Library/Alison Hall: page 107;
Gallo Images/David Hanson: page 27;
Gallo Images/Gavin Hellier: cover;
Great Stock: pages 16, 30, 50;
Valerie Martin: title page, pages 4, 8, 12, 21, 22, 34,
43, 45, 51, 56, 97, 110, 114;
Brian Richards: pages 6, 9, 10, 13, 14, 15, 17, 18, 20,
25, 26, 29, 37, 38, 39, 41, 42, 46, 47, 52, 53, 59, 60, 74,
77, 78, 79, 80, 82, 85, 86, 87, 88, 89, 90, 92, 95, 96, 98,
99, 100, 101, 102, 104, 108, 111, 112, 116, 118, 120;
Neil Setchfield: pages 7, 23, 24, 40, 49, 55;
Travel Ink/Stephen Coyne: page 109;
Travel Ink/Ken Gibson: page 58;
Travel Ink/Simon Reddy: page 28;
Hutchison Library: page 63

Cover: *A view over the Danube River to the stately
Parliament Building, Budapest.*
Title Page: *Colourful painted eggs, a typically
Hungarian craft.*

CONTENTS

1
Introducing Budapest and Hungary

Hungary may be among Europe's smaller nations, yet it packs tremendous variety into its 93,030 km² (35,919 sq miles). The rolling hills of the **north**, the **Great Plain**, the small towns of the **Danube Bend**, the spas of **Transdanubia** and the summer playground of **Lake Balaton** are all within an hour or two's drive of the capital, **Budapest**, itself one of Europe's most attractive and stylish cities.

Throughout the country you will be served splendid cuisine accompanied by some surprisingly good wines in delightfully traditional restaurants. Drive off the main highways and you will sometimes travel for many miles without seeing a single car; if you stick with the railways, a comprehensive network of routes will get you to most places.

Brush up on Hungary's past within these pages and you will have a better understanding of the make-up of this country at the heart of Europe. For Hungary has a history as deep-rooted as any in this part of the world – scratch the surface and you will discover many hidden treasures in its cities, towns and countryside.

Less than a century ago, Hungary was more than double its present size as a constituent part of the **Austro-Hungarian Empire**. The 20th century saw its downsizing in the aftermath of World War I and, 70 years later, its emergence from decades of communism to take its place in a reshaped environment. With membership of the **European Union** imminent, Hungary's future is secure.

Top Attractions

*** Budapest: visit the city's old Castle District; attend a performance at the State Opera House.
*** Esztergom: see the impressive basilica.
*** Lake Balaton: visit Tihany and its Abbey Church.
*** Sopron: wander around the old inner town.
** Hortobágy: the location of the Máta stud farm.
** Eger: a town with fine architecture and a castle.

Opposite: *Traditional costume is worn in Hungary's rural villages.*

FACTS AND FIGURES

• Hungary is 93,030km² (35,919 sq miles) in area – it comprises one per cent of the total area of Europe.
• From west to east, Hungary is 528km (328 miles); from north to south 320km (198 miles). Its border measures 2242km (1393 miles).
• Hungary's highest point is Kékes, in the Mátra Hills, at 1014m (3326ft).
• Lake Balaton is Hungary's largest lake and Europe's largest freshwater lake outside Scandinavia. Its area is 598km² (230 sq miles).
• Hungary's population just exceeds 10 million, of whom 63 per cent live in cities and towns. Budapest's population is two million.

Below: *Lake Balaton is the 'Hungarian sea'.*

THE LAND

Hungary is located within the **Carpathian Basin** in central Europe, bordered by Austria, Slovakia, Ukraine, Romania, Yugoslavia, Croatia and Slovenia. It is split down the middle by the Danube, which enters in the northwest, divides the capital Budapest, and exits in the south near Mohács.

The country has three **topographical** divisions. Almost 75 per cent is low-lying, around 20 per cent is hilly terrain up to 400m (1300ft), and the five per cent above that is mountainous – up to 1000m (3300ft).

The **Great Plain** of the south and east and **Little Plain** in the extreme northwest constitute most of Hungary's lowland area. In the west, Transdanubian uplands include the **Somogy**, **Zala** and **Tolna Hills**; higher still are the Mecsek and central mountain ranges of **Transdanubia** and the **Northern Uplands**.

Approximately 80km (50 miles) to the southwest of Budapest, in the centre of Transdanubia, is **Lake Balaton**, the largest lake in central Europe. It is 77km (48 miles) long and between 1.6km (1 mile) and 14km (9 miles) wide, with an area of 598km² (230 square miles).

Around 1000 **thermal springs** are spread about Hungary, making it the most important country in Europe for spa treatments. The temperature of the mineral-rich water often tops 30°C (86°F), and the benefits are both curative and beautifying.

Regions of Hungary

For visitors who need to find their way about Hungary, the country splits conveniently into **seven regions** – Budapest and surrounds; the

Danube Bend; Lake Balaton and central Transdanubia; Western Transdanubia; Southern Transdanubia; the Great Plain; and the Northern Uplands (or Northeast Hungary).

The capital, **Budapest**, is home to two million people. It straddles the Danube, with its two constituent parts, Buda and Pest, on opposite banks. Some 40km (25 miles) upstream, where the big river takes a 90-degree turn south between hills, is the scenic area called the **Danube Bend**, centred on the towns of Esztergom, Visegrád and Vác.

Above: *View over the capital Budapest towards the Buda Hills.*

Like Budapest, **Lake Balaton** has magnetic visitor appeal and the long, thin lake has spawned a large number of resorts along both its northern and southern shores – these include resorts such as Keszthely, Badacsony, Balatonfüred and Siófok. It's in the middle of Transdanubia, effectively the western two-fifths of the country that lie 'across the Danube'.

North of Lake Balaton is **Western Transdanubia**; south of the lake is **Southern Transdanubia**. The western part is largely hilly, but includes the Little Plain, Hungary's second-largest lowland; the southern part is generally flatter. Main towns in Transdanubia are Győr, Szombathely and Pécs.

The **Great Plain** occupies more than half of Hungary, its flat expanse home to four million Hungarians – the chief cities are Szeged, Kecskemét, Debrecen and Szolnok. To the north, the **Northern Uplands** rising towards the Slovakian border are famous for their wines – especially the Tokaj variety.

THE DANUBE

The Danube, which bisects Hungary, is Europe's second longest river after the Volga, and the principal river of Central Europe. It flows into Hungary at the northwestern tip and leaves it in the south, near Mohács – some 417km (259 miles) of its total 2850km (1770 miles) are in Hungary. The Tisza is Hungary's other main river, with 596km (370 miles) in Hungary; the Dráva, a tributary of the Danube, is Hungary's third longest river.

BUDAPEST	J	F	M	A	M	J	J	A	S	O	N	D
AVERAGE TEMP. °F	30	35	40	53	60	68	70	71	64	53	43	35
AVERAGE TEMP. °C	-1	1	6	12	16	20	21	22	18	12	6	2
HOURS OF SUN DAILY	2	3	5	7	8	9	10	9	7	5	2	1
RAINFALL in	1.5	1.7	1.5	1.8	2.8	2.7	2.2	1.9	1.3	2.2	2.8	1.8
RAINFALL mm	37	44	38	45	72	69	56	47	33	57	70	46
DAYS OF RAINFALL	13	12	11	11	13	13	10	9	7	10	14	13

Above: *The Chain Bridge and River Danube in the heart of Budapest.*

Climate

Hungary sits at the confluence of Europe's key climatic zones, which causes weather patterns to vary from region to region. In the eastern half of the country the climate is broadly **continental**, but in the west and south it is influenced by the **Atlantic** and the **Mediterranean** respectively.

Continental conditions prevail in the **Great Plain**, which has the widest seasonal variations. Summers are hot and dry, with conditions verging on arid; winters are generally cold and often windy. This part of Hungary can sometimes go for long periods without any rainfall, though fierce storms are not unknown in summer.

The climate is similar in the **Northern Uplands**, but with more rain – about 600–800mm (23–31in) against the 500mm (20in) annually in the Great Plain. Late autumn and early winter are the wettest times; snowfall varies from year to year, but is relatively light and does not last very long.

Through **Western Transdanubia** and in **Budapest**, spring's early arrival is followed by a showery May and June and warm summer that can become quite humid in the capital. The July temperature in Budapest averages 21°C (70°F); in January it plummets to –1°C (30°F).

Sunshine levels in Hungary are among the best in Europe, often topping 2000 hours a year. The sunniest part of the country lies between the **Danube** and **Tisza** rivers; the areas with least sun are the Northern Uplands and the Alpine foothills of the west.

HISTORY IN BRIEF

The **Carpathian Basin** – the land south of the Carpathian mountain range in which present-day Hungary sits – has been inhabited since prehistoric times. Shifting borders and invasions by nomadic tribes on the move north from the Balkans characterize part of its history.

In the first few years of Christianity, the **Romans** under Emperor Augustus occupied the area of Hungary south of the Danube and established the province of **Pannonia**, which became the northeastern frontier of their expanding empire – a natural defence against incursions from the east. They established several **garrison towns**, among them Aquincum – on the site of Óbuda suburb in present-day Budapest – which was to become the capital of Lower Pannonia. Other military camps were set up at Pécs (Sophianae), Győr (Arrabona), Sopron (Scarbantia) and Szombathely (Savaria). By the middle of the 2nd century, up to 20,000 soldiers were defending the southern Danube shore between Budapest and Vienna.

With the empire's resources stretched to their limits, Roman withdrawal from Pannonia began in the 4th century – creating a power vacuum in the Carpathian Basin that was seized by the **Huns** under **Attila**. The Huns took Aquincum just before the final Roman pull-out in 430AD, but they capitulated after Attila's death in 453. The **Avars** were among the wave of migrants pushing west; they added the thinly populated territory to the Avar Empire in the 6th century and a period of relative calm ensued before they, too, were conquered.

Marauding Magyars

Seven tribes, involving up to 500,000 people in all and led by **Prince Árpád** – nowadays recognized as

> **THE MAGYARS**
>
> The seven original Magyar tribes originated in Asia rather than Europe, having evolved as an ethnic group between 1000BC and 500BC on the southwestern slopes of the Ural Mountains. The Magyars' first migration from their Magna Hungaria homeland to the Black Sea took place between 700AD and 750AD; around 400,000 strong, they arrived in the Carpathian Basin in 896. Both syllables of the name Magyar – *mogy* and *eri* – mean 'man'; the name Magyar was later adopted by the country and its people.

Below: *Chieftains of the seven Magyar tribes stand proudly at the foot of the Millenary Monument and Colonnade on Heroes' Square in Budapest.*

CHRISTIAN KING

Stephen, Hungary's first Christian king and the founder of the state, inherited the throne from his father, Grand Prince Géza, in 997. He ruled first as grand prince, and from his coronation on Christmas Day 1000 – with a crown requested from and sent by Pope Sylvester II – as king. His legacy included an administrative system of counties and reorganization of the army along Western lines. He was canonized in Székesfehérvár after his death on 15 August 1038; the coronation crown, symbol of the country, is on display in the National Museum (*see* page 50).

the first great Hungarian leader, swept westwards from their home beyond the Urals in 896 and crossed the Carpathians to seize control of the Basin, thus establishing one of the key dates in Hungarian history. They were known collectively as the **Magyars**.

Through much of the 10th century, the Magyars were an ever-present threat to the Christian world. Their raids took them deep into France, Spain, Italy and Germany; also south to Constantinople at the very heart of the Byzantine Empire. The horsemen moved swiftly, plundering and pillaging as they went and repeatedly managing to evade the armies mustered to halt their progress.

The Magyars eventually paid a price for their successes in a decisive defeat by **Henry of Saxony** at Riade, northern Germany, in 933, and again by **King Otto I** at the Battle of Lechfeld, near Augsburg, in 955. Their forces were crushed, their battle plans rendered ineffective by superior Western military tactics.

There were two options for the Magyars – to form themselves into a civilized state or to disappear off the map altogether. **Grand Prince Géza**, great-grandson of Árpád and leader of the Magyars after 972, took the former route – and embraced Christianity.

Kingdom of Hungary

Below: *King Stephen's crown is among Hungary's treasured possessions.*

Catholic missionaries were invited to Hungary and Géza and his son Vajk, who later adopted the Christian name István (Stephen), were baptized.

On Christmas Day in 1000, Stephen was crowned Hungary's first king; papal approval had been sought from Rome and Pope Sylvester II provided the crown at Stephen's request. Under King Stephen I the emergent Christian state began to strengthen its ties with the West.

HISTORICAL CALENDAR

9BC–430AD Roman province of Pannonia extends to Danube.
896 Magyar tribes to seize control of the Carpathian Basin.
955 Magyars defeated by King Otto I at the Battle of Lechfeld.
1000 Stephen crowned first king of a newly Christianized Hungarian state.
1241–42 Mongol invasion devastates the country.
13th century Buda is founded across the Danube from Pest.
1301 Andrew III's death ends rule of the House of Árpád.
1526 After defeat by Suleiman I at Mohács, Hungary is occupied by the Turks for 150 years.
1541 Turks occupy Buda.
1686 Turkish occupation ends after failed attack on Vienna.
1703–11 Rákóczi leads unsuccessful uprising against rule from Vienna.

1740–80 Southeast resettled by Serbs, Romanians and Slavs.
1848–49 Revolution ends in War of Independence. Habsburgs summon Russian aid.
1867 Creation of Austro-Hungarian Empire.
1873 Buda, Pest and Óbuda merge to become Budapest.
1914–18 World War I. Hungary takes German side.
1920 Treaty of Trianon. Hungary surrenders two-thirds of prewar territory to Romania, Czechoslovakia and Yugoslavia.
1939–45 World War II. Hungary involved from June 1941. Nazis invade Hungary in March 1944. Jews deported.
1947 In rigged parliamentary elections, the Communists, led by Mátyás Rákosi, seize power.
1953 Stalin dies, moderate Imre Nagy becomes prime minister.

1956 The Hungarian Uprising. Soviet tanks enter Budapest as Nagy declares neutrality.
1970s Liberalized period of 'goulash Communism' under János Kádár.
1989 Hungary allows East Germans through Iron Curtain. Republic of Hungary proclaimed.
1991 The last Soviet soldiers stationed on Hungarian soil leave in June.
1994 Gyula Horn's Socialist party, the reformed communists, are returned to power by an electorate unhappy at the rate of progress.
1998 Centre-right coalition replaces the Socialists in power.
2000 Hungary applies for membership of the European Union, along with former communist allies Poland and the Czech Republic.

In the 11th and 12th centuries, the Magyars' influence extended over an area three times the country's present size. But the **Mongol invasion** of 1241–42, which wiped out up to 60 per cent of the population in some areas – the only major foreign invasion in the first five centuries of Hungary's existence – brought the country to its knees, and it took a major rebuilding exercise under **Béla IV** to restore some stability. He built castles and founded Buda across the Danube from Pest.

The death of **Andrew III** without an heir in 1301 ended the 400-year rule of the House of Árpád; for the greater part of the next two centuries Hungary was ruled by a succession of foreign kings. For **János Hunyadi**, Hungarian viceroy from 1445–56, there was one main aim in life – to rid Europe of the Turks.

His son, **Matthias Corvinus**, who as king masterminded Hungary's considerable development from 1458–90, helped to mobilize Western support against the Ottoman

HERO OF HUNGARY

The heroics of **Captain Miklós Zrínyi** and his men at Szigetvár, west of Pécs, in 1566 earned him a well deserved place in Hungarian folklore. Zrínyi was in charge of a 2400-strong Hungarian and Croatian army who defended Szigetvár ('island castle') in a 33-day siege by 100,000 Ottoman troops under Suleiman I intent on taking Vienna. Denied Habsburg support, Zrínyi and his men launched a final act of self-sacrifice against the Turks, in which most of them died; Suleiman also perished in the conflict, along with 20,000 of the Turkish force.

Empire, which by 1520 was five times the size of Hungary.

Defeat by the Turks

Though Matthias Corvinus enjoyed some military success against the invading Turks, the Hungarians suffered badly at the hands of **Sultan Suleiman I** (Suleiman the Magnificent) in 1526. The young **King Louis II** died in the decisive battle at Mohács, in the south of Hungary.

Turkish occupation

of Buda followed in 1541 and, with the nation in disarray, Hungary became split into three parts for the next century and a half. The centre of the country was incorporated into the **Ottoman Empire**; Eastern Hungary became a separate **Transylvanian principality** under Turkish control; while what was left of the Kingdom of Hungary in the north and west was occupied by the **Habsburgs** – effectively creating a buffer zone to keep the Turkish armies from moving on Western Europe.

Previously united Hungary thus became little more than an unsettled frontier zone between the Habsburg and Ottoman empires, disrupted by frequent hostile skirmishes between the two opposing factions and with a decidedly bleak future.

Life was harsh under Turkish occupation. The Medieval settlements fell into disuse and large-scale tree felling destroyed the delicate ecological balance of the Great Plain region, turning much of the area into unproductive marshland.

With Turkish influence on the wane in the late 17th century, the Hungarians increased their stance against the Habsburgs. However, peace in the region was still very much far from reality.

MATTHIAS CORVINUS

King Matthias Corvinus, who ruled from 1458 until 1490, presided over a golden era of Hungarian civic and cultural advancement. He taxed the nobility to pay for a mercenary Black Army of up to 30,000 men which maintained Hungary's status as a leading central European power. He also made overtures of peace to the threatening Turks that bought time while he developed his defences. His second wife, Queen Beatrice, brought workers and craftsmen from Italy to enhance the palace of Visegrád – said at the time to be Europe's most splendid royal seat – and the Royal Palace in Buda.

Under the Habsburgs

The Turks' failed attack on Vienna in 1683 was one incursion too many and brought the curtain down on their Hungarian episode. It also united the Christian powers and in 1686 they retook Buda Castle, which had been occupied by the Turks. Within two years, the Ottoman presence in Hungary was all but over.

Opposition to the Habsburgs was growing and the 1703–11 uprising by the nobility and peasants proved a long, drawn-out and ultimately unsuccessful protest at rule from Vienna. Though the Transylvanian prince **Ferenc Rákóczi II** had succeeded in uniting Hungarians against Habsburg rule, in the end Hungary was no more than a province of the Habsburg empire.

As such it made great progress, however. **Empress Maria Theresa**, the Habsburg ruler from 1740–80, and her son **Joseph II** (1780–90) oversaw a period of enlightenment in Hungary during which the foundations of industry were laid and the depopulated southeast resettled by Serbs, Romanians and Slavs.

Some 90 per cent of the population was still scraping a living on the land at this time. Hints by the aristocracy of imminent reforms failed to make an impression, leading to a new independence struggle in the mid-19th century.

Independence Struggle

The revolution of 1848–49 that ended in the War of Independence began with a **rebellion** in March 1848.

Led by the Hungarian poet **Sándor Petőfi**, it called for wide-ranging reforms – everything from establishing a responsible government to freedom of the press and the abolition of serfdom.

The struggle for liberation continued throughout 1848 and into 1849. **Count Lajos Batthyány**, prime

---

PEASANTS' REVOLT

The death of King Matthias Corvinus in 1490 signalled the end of a progressive era for Hungary. The nobility accelerated their exploitation of the peasants, who rose up against landlord oppression in 1514 under the leadership of György Dózsa. More than 70,000 were tortured and killed and Dózsa was burned alive. The Tripartium Law drawn up by István Verboczy, a nobleman, served to reiterate the nobles' privileges over the exploited serfs.

Opposite: *The mounted King Stephen is one of Budapest's finest statues.*
Below: *Fascinating old buildings line the streets of Budapest's Castle District.*

DAYS OF EMPIRE

The Austro-Hungarian Empire occupied a significant chunk of present-day Central Europe. Hungary's borders extended as far as Belgrade in the south and incorporated Transylvania, now part of Romania. It also embraced Croatia, which conducted its affairs independently within the Hungarian kingdom. The Austrian part of the empire extended from Trieste and the Tyrol to Prague and parts of present-day Ukraine.

Below: *Heroes of 1956 were tried in Budapest's Military Court of Justice.*

minister of the newly installed independent Hungarian government, organized a national guard that provided the foundation of Hungary's independent army.

Habsburg forces attacked Hungary in September 1848, and in April 1849 parliament decamped from Buda to Debrecen; journalist-turned-statesman **Lajos Kossuth** was elected leader of the provisional government, which declared Hungary's full independence from the Habsburgs.

In August 1849 came the Austrian retribution. **Emperor Franz Joseph I** sought assistance from the Russian **Czar Nicholas I**, who supplied 200,000 men to crush a Hungarian army weakened by the defection of some ethnic minorities from the freedom cause.

In 1867, a compromise arrangement with the Habsburgs aimed at stemming demand for home rule created the **Austro-Hungarian Empire**, in which Hungary had self-government while sharing the defence and foreign ministries with the Austrians.

It was under the so-called Dual Monarchy that Budapest's development took place. In 1873, the three cities of Buda, Pest and Óbuda – jointly home to about 300,000 people – were merged to form the nation's capital, **Budapest**.

World War I

As part of the Austro-Hungarian federation, Hungarians were forced to fight on the German Empire's side in World War I. They entered the war in July 1914, exactly one month after the murder of the Habsburg **Archduke Franz Ferdinand** in Sarajevo. Hundreds of thousands of Hungarians perished on the Russian and Italian fronts.

The dismantling of the Habsburg Empire was inevitable after the war and, under the **Treaty of Trianon** (4 June 1920), Hungary was forced to surrender two-thirds of its prewar territory to neighbouring countries – Romania, Czechoslovakia and Yugoslavia. The Hungarian population fell from 18 million to 7.6 million. Most harshly felt was the loss of Transylvania, with its population of 1.7 million Magyars, to Romania. Trianon placed some 3.3 million ethnic Hungarians outside Hungary's borders.

The social democrat government of **Mihály Károlyi**, set up soon after the war, was short-lived. In March 1919 the Communists, led by **Béla Kun**, seized power and established a Republic of Councils, which set out to nationalize land and industry. But opposition grew and the regime collapsed when Romanian troops took control of Budapest.

With the Communist 'red terror' gone, a 'white terror' purge of Jews and Communists ensued as fascism took hold with the election of **Admiral Miklós Horthy** as regent in charge of the 'kingdom without a king'.

Above: *Large fields of sunflowers paint the landscape yellow in Northern Hungary.*

WORKING THE LAND

Between the two world wars, Hungary was a largely agrarian nation, with more than half the population involved in the cultivation of crops. However, the holdings of the self-employed were so small – less than 5ha (12.4 acres) – that they scarcely supported the families who farmed them. Land reform after World War II did little to ease rural hardship; the collectivization of agriculture under communist rule saw a gradual drift away from the land.

Above: *Hungary's Jews were forced by the Nazis to wear a yellow Star of David.*

Horthy to World War II

Under Horthy's imposition of traditionalist values on the depleted Hungarian population, the peasants were forced into an even tougher existence. The move to regain lands that had been forfeited under the Trianon Treaty strengthened in the 1930s, and Hungary's right-wing leadership sought assistance from Germany and Italy.

After the outbreak of World War II in September 1939, Hungary called on **Nazi support** to secure the return of northern Transylvania by Romania in July 1940 and a portion of Croatia the following year – but at an enormous price.

By June 1941, Hungary was embroiled in a war that was to prove as costly to the country in human terms as the 1914–18 conflict. Hungarian soldiers joined the **Axis forces** in the invasion of the USSR in 1941, and the casualty list on the retreat from Stalingrad in 1943 was high – during the course of World War II, Hungary lost some 140,000 soldiers.

The government of prime minister **Miklós Kallay** courted the Allies in a bid to balance ties with the Germans, but Hitler was less than impressed. The Nazis invaded Hungary in March 1944 and Horthy was pressurized into installing the **Nazi Arrow Cross** fascist regime under **Ferenc Szálasi** – which promptly set about deporting Hungary's Jewish population to labour camps (*see* panel, this page).

By Christmas 1944, the Red Army had surrounded Budapest. A siege of the capital followed and the Germans eventually fled Hungary in April 1945. By that time, only a quarter of Budapest's buildings were left intact and every Danube bridge had been destroyed.

THE FATE OF THE JEWS

Hungarian citizens of Jewish origin, having suffered persecution from 1940 onwards, became victims of the Nazi Arrow Cross Party after the German invasion of Hungary on 19 March 1944. The Nazis passed anti-Jewish laws similar to those in Germany forcing the Jews to wear a yellow Star of David; they were herded into ghettos and deported. Half of the 800,000 Jews living in war-affected Hungary perished in labour camps like Auschwitz or were killed by the Arrow Cross in 1944.

Under the Communists

By November 1945, the way to democracy looked clear, with the staging of free elections in which the independent **Smallholders Party** gained a majority. But the Soviets insisted on the formation of a coalition government and through rigged parliamentary elections in 1947 the Communists, led by **Mátyás Rákosi**, seized power. The multiparty system collapsed and the Communists and Social Democrats merged to become the **Hungarian Socialist Workers' Party**.

Typical in a totalitarian 'people's republic' was the emergence of the dreaded **secret police** (ÁVO), who gathered their so-called evidence for show trials – everybody feared for their lives.

There was feuding within the Communist party and interior minister **László Rajk** was executed in 1949 as Rákosi followed the hard Stalinist line.

Peasants were herded into collective farms, whose produce went to the state. Half a million Hungarians became victims of the ÁVO-imposed political terror and many of them were ordered into the forced labour camps.

After Stalin's death in 1953, Moscow's more moderate leadership replaced prime minister Rákosi with the moderate Communist **Imre Nagy** (*see* panel, this page). Unfortunately, Nagy's reform plans were blocked by the old guard and he was kicked out of the party, but the seeds of anti-regime protest had been sown, first in literature and then in debates. Increasing disatisfaction led to the Hungarian Uprising of 1956.

> **IMRE NAGY**
>
> Imre Nagy, Hungarian prime minister from 1953–55, was the key figure at the centre of the 1956 Uprising. Frustrated in his reform efforts, he was expelled from the Communist Party in 1955 but readmitted a year later. During 1956, student calls in Budapest and Szeged to have him reinstated as prime minister sparked the uprising. For a few days Nagy led a hastily formed government of neutrality before the Soviet tanks rolled in. He was among 2000 people executed in the aftermath of the revolt and died on 16 June 1958 after a secret trial.

Below: *Imre Nagy statue recalls the man at the centre of the 1956 Uprising.*

HUNGARIANS ABROAD

For every 10 Hungarians living in Hungary, there are four living in other parts of the world. Besides Hungary's population of 10 million-plus, there are 3.2 million ethnic Hungarians in the countries of the Carpathian basin, including two million in Romania, 650,000 in Yugoslavia and Croatia, and 600,000 in Slovakia. There are 700,000 Hungarians living in the USA, 100,000 in Canada, 40,000 in Australia and 25,000 in the UK.

The 1956 Uprising

What started as a student demonstration on 23 October 1956 in support of reforms in Poland quickly became one of support for Nagy and escalated into the major uprising that cost many lives and caused some 200,000 Hungarians to flee to the West.

Within days, Nagy had installed an interim coalition government; by 1 November he had issued a declaration of neutrality and withdrawal from the Warsaw Pact. This action brought swift reprisals. Soviet reinforcements crossed the Hungarian border on 1 November and three days later, with the West preoccupied by the Suez crisis, tanks lumbered into Budapest.

As the street fighting raged, a new government was installed under the leadership of former interior minister

János Kádár, who had defected from Nagy's interim government to join the Russians. The communists restored one-party rule and reprisals followed. Under Kádár, Hungary trod a more liberalized path within the communist framework. 'Those not against us are with us', was Kádár's most telling phrase, reversing Stalin's old maxim. The era of 'goulash communism', with its greater consumerism, reflected a relaxed interpretation of Soviet doctrine within the Hungarian camp – it was socialism with a human face.

The standard of living made huge strides in the 1970s and by the 1980s, with **foreign investment** increasingly forthcoming, Hungary was perceived as 'the Soviet bloc country with one foot in the West'.

The Curtain Comes Down

By the end of the 1980s, the Soviet Union was digesting Gorbachev's glasnost and perestroika – a powerful cocktail that burned a hole in the socialist world order and led to the destruction of the Soviet Union itself.

The events of 1956 were by now seen as a 'popular uprising' rather than a 'counter-revolution'. And when prime minister **Miklós Nemeth** was among the many attending the reburial of Imre Nagy and his 1956 associates on 16 June 1989, the writing was on the wall.

In September 1989, Nemeth's government allowed East German refugees to escape to the West through Austria – the first stage of communism's collapse in eastern Europe. The following month, exactly 33 years after the uprising, the **Republic of Hungary** was proclaimed, and in October 1990 the communists were crushed by a centre-right coalition led by **József Antall** in the first multi-party elections.

After 40 years of Soviet-dominated inertia, Hungarians were impatient for progress. Within five years of the Iron Curtain's collapse, the reformed communists had been elected into power in a coalition with the Free Democrats.

This was no return to the bad old days, however. The Hungarian Socialist Party, having disowned its past, had in opposition helped to lay the foundations of democracy.

Throughout the 1990s, Hungary further strengthened its trade ties with countries of the former Western Europe and in 2000 applied to join the 15-country European Union, seeing its future in a united Europe. It expects to be accepted for membership by 2005.

GOVERNMENT AND ECONOMY

To those who had visited Hungary in the late 1980s, the country's role in the dismantling of communism came as little surprise – both economically and mentally, Hungary had displayed its independence from Communist ideology.

Above: *The red, white and green Hungarian flag.*
Opposite: *This memorial in Szolnok pays tribute to those who died in the Hungarian Uprising.*

LIBERAL LEADER

When János Kádár – who had served in Imre Nagy's government – joined the Communists and was made prime minister in September 1956, with Soviet tanks still on Budapest's streets, he was the most reviled man in Hungary. But though Kádár served as prime minister from 1956–58 and 1961–65, his liberal policies improved the standard of living among Hungary's people. Under Kádár, Hungary embraced 'market socialism' and became known as 'the most cheerful barracks in the socialist camp'. Unable to deal with soaring inflation and a growing national debt, he was dismissed in 1988 and died the next year aged 77.

Above: *The Hungarian Parliament sits in session.*
Opposite: *Hungary's rich folk traditions live on in colourful costumes worn for special occasions.*

SAY IT IN HUNGARIAN

Pronunciation of Hungarian is consistent – each vowel and consonant always sounds the same. The stress is always on the first syllable, which can result in something of a monotone. Note that **cs**, **gy**, **sz** and **zs** are regarded as single letters. Here are some consonants:

c as *ts* in bats
cs as *ch* in lurch
gy as *j* in jury
j as *y* in yes
ly as *y* in yes
ny as *ch* in vineyard
s as *sh* in shop
sz as *s* in seat
ty as *tu* in Tuesday
zs as *s* in measure

The most liberally minded of the old Eastern Bloc countries, Hungary had already succeeded in attracting a degree of Western investment. When the **Iron Curtain** finally fell, Hungary's economy was prepared for the privatization of its industry.

Despite glowing visions of immediate prosperity, however, growth in the early years proved difficult. As in the other former satellite states of the Soviet Union, the early 1990s saw Hungarians struggling to come to terms with the fact that they had been better off under the communist regime.

A nation used to the protectionist and isolationist policies of the communists for a period of 40 years, they found the reality of a **market economy** unbelievably harsh – even though Hungary had started introducing reforms that set it apart from other eastern European states back in the 1960s.

Exacerbating the problem were economic difficulties among Hungary's former Eastern Bloc trading partners and the **general recession** of the time. Hitherto a little-used word in the Hungarian vocabulary, **unemployment** now soared to Western proportions – from 0.5 per cent to 12.5 per cent between 1989 and 1993.

Privatization continued apace through the 1990s towards the 100 per cent level demanded by the government, at first involving foreign investors and then also embracing local investment. Over the past decade, Hungary has received the lion's share of foreign funding that has been ploughed into countries of the now defunct **East European Comecon** trading group.

Development of new foreign markets has been crucial to Hungary's industrial revival in the latter 1990s – the production of vehicles, pharmaceuticals and electronic goods are among key industries now. **Communications** have taken a turn for the better, with improved roads and a modernized telephone system now in place.

The spur for Hungary's economic improvement has been the country's drive for membership of the **European Union**, with whose members Hungary conducts more than 60 per cent of its foreign trade. Hungary, with Poland and the Czech Republic, constitute the next wave of EU hopefuls and the first involving former Iron Curtain countries – they could all be accepted as early as 2004.

Meanwhile, the political spectrum has narrowed after the initial post-communism euphoria that saw the rise to varying degrees of prominence of parties such as the Hungarian Democratic Forum, Christian Democrats, Smallholders and Young Democrats' Federation.

With the extremes of right or left having been endured for most of the past 60 years, Hungary's immediate political future now appears to lie in a more **centrist** government, whethers a single party or power-sharing coalition.

> **SOME LIKE IT HOT**
>
> The long strands of dark red and orange paprikas you see hanging out to dry are the very trademark of Hungarian cuisine, yet paprika is not Hungarian in origin. **Paprika** is said by some to have been brought back from the Americas by Christopher Columbus; others say it arrived with the Turkish invaders. It is now popular both as a pickled or fresh vegetable, and also in powdered form for the seasoning of dishes.

SERVICES IN ENGLISH

Church services in English are
held at a number of churches
within Budapest. They include:
Baptist – International
Baptist Church, Törökvész út
48 (Buda II). Sunday 10.00.
Interdenominational –
International Church of
Budapest, Óbuda Community
Centre, Kis Korona utca 7
(Buda III). Sunday 10.30.
Presbyterian – Church of
Scotland, Vörösmarty utca
51 (Pest VI). Sunday 11.00.
Roman Catholic – Pesti
Jézus Szíve Templom, Mária
utca 25 (Pest VIII). Mass
Saturday 17.00.

Below: *Musical tradition
is alive and well in all parts
of Hungary.*

THE PEOPLE

Hungary's **population** has been in decline for the past
two decades and now numbers around 10.2 million. This
figure includes an estimated 400,000 Romanies (gypsies)
and 200,000 Germans – plus Romanians, Slovaks, Serbs
and Croats.

From the Magyar conquest onwards, Hungary has
welcomed foreign settlers and today they live mainly in
the border regions. The ethnic minorities have rights
enshrined under Hungarian law. The **Hungarian con-
stitution** guarantees freedom and equality – and the free
use of language – to the country's 22 ethnic minorities
and 82 Romany organizations.

Meanwhile, some five million Magyars live outside
Hungary's borders, with the Transylvania region of
Romania home to more than two million of them.
Magyars also live in Slovakia, Yugoslavia, Croatia
and Ukraine.

Life expectancy among Hungarian men is low by
European standards at 68 years; a decade ago it was
just 65, with only 54 per cent
reaching that age. Women can
expect to live eight years longer –
and are noticeably in the majority
in Hungary.

Transdanubia and Budapest
were first to feel the **modernizing**
influences of Western Europe – in
contrast to the eastern part of the
country, where traditions are deeply
rooted and the old Hungarian character – shaped by pride, vanity and
commitment to freedom – is still
very much in evidence.

Education

Hungarians can trace their education system back more than 1000
years. The first seat of learning was
founded as far back as 996AD by

Benedictine monks at their monastery in the Transdanubian village of **Pannonhalma**.

The first **universities** in Hungary evolved in Pécs in 1367 and Óbuda – now part of Budapest – in 1395. Not until the late 18th century, however, were the foundations laid for a unified schooling system in terms of curriculum and organization. Latin gave way to Hungarian as the language of learning in the mid-19th century.

Today, Hungarian children may attend nursery school from the age of three to six. Education is compulsory from six to 16 – at primary school level until 14, followed by four years in grammar or technical secondary school, or two to three years in a training or vocational school.

Above: *The high dome of St Stephen's Basilica.*

Religion

Hungary celebrated its Christian millennium in 2000 – 1000 years after the acceptance by its first king, Stephen I, of a papal crown that strengthened growing ties with **Catholicism**. The country remained wholly Catholic until the arrival of **Orthodox Romanians** in the 13th and 14th centuries.

The Reformation and Counter-Reformation under the Habsburgs in the 16th and 17th centuries further shifted the denominational structure and Catholicism continued to dominate – today it accounts for 70 per cent of the population. Around 20 per cent of Hungarians claim affiliation to the protestant **Hungarian Reformed Church** and 5 per cent are **Lutheran**.

Other **religious groups** practising in Hungary today include the Baptists, Methodists, Nazarenes, Seventh Day Adventists, Mormons and the Evangelical Pentecostal Fellowship.

WELL ADDRESSED

Addresses in Budapest need a little explanation. The Roman numeral preceding the street indicates the district of the city (given in the At A Glance section as Buda I, Pest V, etc., to show which side of the river it is). The address V Szalay u. 6 III/14 translates as No. 6 Szalay utca (street); III is the floor number and 14 the apartment number. The two middle numbers of the four-digit Budapest postal code relate to the city district – thus an address ending 1051 Budapest is in V District.

Above: *Ornate postbox in central Budapest.*

Language

Hungarian is among Europe's oldest languages, spoken by 15 million people. It's also one of the most difficult to learn. As its closest relatives are Finnish and Estonian in the Finno-Ugric branch of the Uralic linguistic grouping, you are unlikely to understand much of what you hear.

Ethnic groups within Hungary's borders do not have **dialects** to worry about and communication doesn't usually present a problem. Hungarians are not the world's greatest linguists, however, so making yourself understood will probably require a certain degree of patience.

For the vast majority of visitors who don't speak Hungarian, **German** is the best alternative; **English** is understood reasonably well in Budapest, but less so outside the capital. However, if you are determined to attempt a little basic Hungarian, your efforts will be most appreciated.

Literature

The first Hungarian to have had international literary impact was the poet **Sándor Petőfi** (1823–49), leader of the rebellion of March 1848 that led to the War of Independence. His friend **János Arany** (1817–82) was a prominent Romantic poet who also drew inspiration from folk songs.

Endre Ady (1877–1919) is credited with being the founder of modern Hungarian poetry; **Attila József** (1905–37) was another whose writings inspired debate. More recently, **Gyula Illyés** (1902–83) was prominent among the poets.

Important modern authors include **György Konrád** (b 1933), **Péter Nádas** (b 1942), **György Petri** (b 1943) and **Péter Esterházy** (b 1950). Konrád's contribution has been of particular value in providing a literary record of Hungarian history. Finding quality English translations may be difficult, however.

Drama

Though Hungarian theatre has its origins in the 11th century, it was during the 1500s that theatrical performances became popular at the Royal Court. Stage companies came into being at the end of the 18th century, and in 1837 the **National Theatre** was founded in Budapest.

The theatre regularly stages works by leading Hungarian dramatists – **József Katona**, **Mihály Vörösmarty** and **Imre Madách** among them. The theatre premiered Madách's *The Tragedy of Man* on 21 September 1883; by way of celebration, 21 September was made the **Day of Hungarian Drama**.

Hungary's film industry, which took off in the silent days pre-1920, has maintained a steady output. Among its leading figures is producer **István Szabó**, who was awarded an Oscar for *Mephisto* in 1982.

Art

Many prominent Hungarian painters have their work displayed in the **Hungarian National Gallery** in Budapest. Among them are the Romantics **Bertalan Székely** (1835–1910), who created the Mohács piece *Recovering the Corpse of the King*, and **Gyula Benczúr** (1844–1920), with *Recapture of Buda Castle*.

In the field of Realism, **Mihály Munkácsy** (1844–1900) was a noted landscape painter who focused on the *puszta* (*see* page 105); several of his paintings sombrely captured events from the War of Independence.

The turn-of-the-century Hungarian art scene was dominated by **Kosztka Tivadar Csontváry** (1853–1919), whose works included *The Ruins of the Greek Theatre of Taormina*, *Baalbek* and *The Lonely Cedar Tree*, and the portrait painter **József Rippl-Rónai** (1861–1927), among whose creations is *Maiden with the Cage*.

> ### THE SOUND OF FOLK
>
> Folk music is very much alive in Hungary and the *táncház* (dance house) is where it all happens. You'll find them in Budapest and towns around Hungary. The range of instruments used in traditional folk music is wide – *cimbalom* (an unusual stringed instrument played with a stick), violin, bagpipe, zither, hurdy-gurdy and lute among them. Learn one or two of the lively Hungarian dances while you're there. Folk music should not be confused with gypsy music, which stems from the *verbunkos* (soldiers' recruitment tunes) and is performed in restaurants throughout the land.

Below: *The Matthias Church in Budapest has fine stained glass.*

Opposite: *Immersed in the game of chess.*
Below: *The State Opera House is known for its sumptuous interior.*

Music

Hungarian music takes its place on the world stage primarily through the efforts of three composers – **Franz (Ferenc) Liszt** (1811–86), **Béla Bartók** (1881–1945) and **Zoltán Kodály** (1882–1967).

Through his compositions infusing Hungarian tradition with Romanticism, Liszt became a highly popular figure throughout Europe in the mid-1800s. He was instrumental in Hungary's musical evolution, founding the **Academy of Music** in Budapest.

Bartók and Kodály both found prominence through their blending of traditional Hungarian folk forms into their individual musical styles. Together they made a tremendous impact on 20th-century Hungarian music.

Ferenc Erkel (1810–93) introduced his native Hungarian language to the **opera** stage. His best-known works, regularly performed in Budapest's Opera House, which he founded, are *Hunyadi László* and *Bánk Bán*.

Architecture

Baroque dominates pre-19th-century architectural style in Hungary and many fine examples exist – **Tihany's Abbey Church** by Lake Balaton is among the finest creations. A smaller selection of **Gothic** and **Romanesque** pieces also exist.

Hungary's architectural revolution of the late 19th century saw the emergence of an eclectic style: in Budapest, **Imre Steindl** designed the Parliament Building, **Frigyes Schulek** created the Fisherman's Bastion and **Ignác Alpár** built the fairytale Vajdahunyad Castle in Városliget (City Park).

Ödön Lechner's secessionist creations of the period included the capital's **Museum of Applied Arts**; Lechner went on to establish a style of typically Hungarian architecture using glazed tiles from Pécs. To the fore among modern Hungarian architects is **Imre Makovecz**, who has advanced his own 'organic architecture'.

Sport and Recreation

Hungary is an **equestrian** nation and abundant opportunities exist in all parts of the country both for trail riding and for tutoring novices and advanced riders alike. The greatest concentration of equestrian facilities can be found around Lake Balaton and on the Great Plain.

Lake Balaton offers unrivalled variety for outdoor pursuits. **Dinghy sailing** has been popular there for well over a century; conditions are ideally suited and on summer weekends the sails of hundreds of yachts can be seen. Dinghies can be hired by the day or for an hour or two – as can boards for **windsurfing**.

You can also hire a bicycle and pedal off along the edge of Lake Balaton; some 220km (136 miles) of **cycle tracks** are now open and new stretches are being added each year, eventually to link up all around the lake.

There is plenty of scope for cycling in Hungary – over stiff gradients in the Northern Uplands, across less demanding terrain in Transdanubia, and over the vast and often windy flat expanse of the Great Plain.

Fishing is a big attraction in the early and late summer, for the *fogas* (pike-perch) for which Balaton is known, and also for carp – both can weigh up to 10kg (22lb). The Tisza River in the east of the country is another prime angling location.

NATIONAL ANTHEM

The 'Anthem' poem written by Ferenc Kölcsey in 1823, with music to accompany it composed by Ferenc Erkel in 1844, is Hungary's national anthem by statute since 23 October 1989. There are eight verses, of which only the first is used for official occasions, as follows:
Bless the Magyar, O our God,
Bountifully, gladly.
Shield with Thy protecting hand
When his foes smite madly.
Fate, of old, has rent him sore;
May it now bring healing.
Bygone sins are all atoned,
Even the future sealing.

Above: *The Magyars were responsible for introducing mouthwatering goulash.*
Opposite: *Hungarian wines are top-quality.*

GO FOR GOULASH

Forget the goulash you've eaten at home – authentic Hungarian **gulyás**, as introduced by the Magyars, is altogether different. In its original form, *gulyás* is an extremely filling thick soup containing meat, small potatoes, onion, peppers and tomato, liberally spiced with paprika and garlic, and intended as a main course. The *gulyás* you eat outside Hungary is called *pörkölt*, or meat stew, by the Hungarians; another variation is *tokány*, with sour cream and different vegetables.

Food and Drink

Hungary is not the best place to be in the world for vegetarian visitors or those who are on a strict diet. But it does offer a wide variety of interesting and exciting ethnic flavours to sharpen the jaded palate.

Reggeli (**breakfast**) can consist of just a roll and a cup or two of good strong coffee, or otherwise it can include a full-blown plate of meat, cheese and eggs, and may sometimes even be helped down by an early morning *pálinka*, the powerful local brandy.

Though *ebéd* (**lunch**) is traditionally the main meal of the day for Hungarians, you can choose to dine just as copiously in the **evening** *(vácsora)*. You will never be left wanting more – Hungarian food is solid and filling, the ample dishes often traceable back to peasant origins.

Hungarians are a nation of great **meat** eaters, with pork being the most popular meat of choice. But beef, veal, wild boar, venison, turkey, chicken, pheasant, duck and goose can all be found gracing menus, too. Small dumpling-sized **noodles**, called *galuska*, often accompany the meal.

Fish is plentiful, especially around Lake Balaton – the local *fogas* (pike-perch) is a tasty delicacy, and carp, pike and trout abound. Speciality fish dishes include *paprikás ponty* (carp in paprika sauce) and *pisztráng tejszín mártásban* (trout baked in cream).

The word *mártás* is Hungarian for **sauce**, of which there are many to accompany your meat or fish – among them *bormártás* (wine sauce), *fokhagymás mártás* (garlic sauce), *meggymártás* (cherry sauce) and *gombamártás* (mushroom sauce).

Paprika is widely used and is a common ingredient in many Hungarian meals. It comes in several degrees of piquancy, from mild to hot – whatever your feelings about the spice, it adds a quintessentially Hungarian character to any meal.

But first, the starter. Hungary is rich in *levesek* (**soups**) of all kinds, and you are bound to sample *gulyásleves* (*see* panel, page 28). At Lake Balaton and along the Tisza River around Szeged, the emphasis switches to **fish** and *halászlé* – a spicy, paprika-laden fish stew with giant lumps of pike-perch and carp; it's often cooked in a mini-cauldron and can be taken as a main course.

Other soups include *jókai bableves* (bean soup with smoked meat) and *újházi tyúkleves* (chicken soup with noodles) – also **cold soups** that go down well in summer, like *meggyleves* (cold sour cherry soup).

When it comes to **dessert**, the Hungarian *rétes* (strudel) is well worth saving space for, filled either with apple, sour cherry or cottage cheese. Also delicious is the *gundel palacsinta*, a flambéed pancake with nuts and raisins covered in a chocolate and rum sauce.

Hungarian **wines** can be of excellent quality, the best-known among them being *Tokaj* (*see* panel, page 120). Outstanding white wines are produced on the northern slopes above Lake Balaton and you are sure to try *Egri Bikavér*, the deep red 'Bull's Blood' produced from several varieties of grape.

> ### COFFEE AND CAKE
>
> The *cukrászda* (Hungarian patisserie) caters for the Hungarians' sweet tooth and is often part of a larger chandelier-decked coffee house where you can gorge on sticky strudel, well-filled pancakes or anything from the inevitably impressive display of cakes and pastries. Get your tongue round a *dobostorta* (chocolate and cream cake with a topping of brown sugar and caramel). To follow, there's strong espresso coffee (ask for milk to dilute), maybe cappuccino and usually tea. Gerbeaud, founded in 1884, is Budapest's best-known coffee house.

2
Budapest

Budapest is home to two million people – one in five Hungarians lives in this capivating city on the Danube which, with its colourful past, presents itself as one of the truly great European capitals. The city came into being in 1873 with the merging of **Buda**, **Pest** and **Óbuda**, though the three parts have retained their identities through the decades. Budapest is one of the best cities in Europe for orientation, with the Danube cutting a swathe between hilly Buda to the west and flat Pest, with its wide boulevards, to the east. The oldest part of Budapest, Óbuda, is now a suburb on the Buda side of the river to the north.

If you have only a couple of days in Budapest, spend at least a morning in the Castle District. If you're in town for a week, devote a couple of days to the area. That will give you time to fully explore the **Royal Palace**, amble along the district's cobbled streets, investigate the collection of private **museums**, admire the **architecture** of 18th- and 19th-century Baroque houses in the streets, and sample traditional Hungarian cooking in a selection of welcoming **restaurants**.

To reach the Castle District from the Pest side of the Danube, cross the **Chain Bridge** and take the **Budavári Sikló** funicular railway – it dates from the 19th century – or climb the stairs leading up through the trees from Clark Adám tér. Alternatively you can catch metro line 2 to the Moszkva tér public transport intersection and take the Várbusz (identified by its castle symbol in place of a route number) on Várfok utca, or take bus 16 from Deák Ferenc tér in Pest to Disz tér by the Royal Palace.

DON'T MISS

*** Buda's Castle District: stroll around the narrow streets and visit the Matthias Church on Castle Hill.
*** Parliament Building: go on a tour of this magnificent edifice.
*** State Opera House: make sure you attend a performance here.
*** The Royal Palace: visit its museums and art galleries.
** Fisherman's Bastion: a fine view towards Parliament.
** St Stephen's Basilica: has a relic of the saint-king.
** Danube River cruise: a different city perspective.

Opposite: *Colour in the costumes and the Matthias Church roof.*

BUDA

Matthias Church **

You will have seen the church dominating the Castle District from across the river. This is the Matthias Church, with its distinctive, coloured roof tiles, on Szentháromság tér (Holy Trinity Square) next to the Hilton Hotel.

The church looks older than it is – mostly a neo-Gothic design of the late 19th century by architect **Frigyes Schulek**. It was named after the 15th-century Renaissance king and incorporates parts of a 13th-century church that once occupied the site.

On your left through the solid wooden doors is the **coat of arms** of King Matthias, who married Beatrice of Aragon here; at its centre the raven and ring representing the family name Corvinus.

The church's richly painted **interior** has few equals – pillars, walls, arches and vaulting of dark red and gold motifs beneath a canopy of blue and gold. Large **frescoes** occupy the spaces between the abstract geometrics on the walls, mostly the work of **Károly Lotz** and

Bertalan Székely, two eminent Romantic painters of the day.

The **crypt** (which has a small admission charge) contains ecclesiastical exhibits; from here stairs lead up to the highly decorated **St Stephen's Chapel**, at its entrance a bust of Queen Elizabeth (1837–98), known as 'Sissy', by **György Zala**.

It was in St Matthias Church, at the coronation of Emperor Franz Josef I and Elizabeth as king and queen of Hungary in 1867, that Franz Liszt's *Coronation Mass* was first performed, having been composed specifically for the occasion.

Up a narrow staircase is the **Royal Oratory**, where replicas of Hungary's crown jewels – King Stephen's crown, orb and sceptre – are displayed and the making of the crown explained in detail. Robes and chalices line an upper gallery.

Above: *The fairytale towers of the Fisherman's Bastion above the Danube.*

Fisherman's Bastion ★★

Behind the church, the fairytale structure with its five turrets flanking a main tower is the Fisherman's Bastion, built in 1890–1905 by **Schulek** as a promenade from which to admire his ecclesiastical work on one side and the fine view along the Danube on the other. Upstream are the Buda Hills and green Margaret Island, across the river the best view to be had of the Parliament building, and to your right, on the opposite bank beyond the Chain Bridge, a clutch of riverside five-star hotels – the Atrium Hyatt, Inter-Continental and Marriott.

Fishermen from the Víziváros district below the hill were said to have defended this area in the Middle Ages; it was also the site of a fish market. By the bastion is a splendid **equestrian statue** of King Stephen wearing both crown and halo – it is widely held to be the finest of all the capital's statues.

GO WALKABOUT

Guided walks with English language commentary show visitors the best of Budapest. **The Gems of Buda Castle** explores the architectural styles of the Castle District, from the Royal Palace to the Vienna Gate (departs from Matthias Church 14:30 daily). Other walks leave the Café Gerbeaud on Vörösmarty tér at 10:30 daily, taking in sights on the **Pest** side of the river. Details from **Robinson Travel**, tel: 340 4232. Other walking tours: **Blue Guide Tours**, tel: 316 8376; **I. A. Tours**, tel: 211 8861; **Kontroll Travel**, tel: 267 8566; and **Paul Street Tours**, tel: 958 2545.

CHILD'S PLAY

Head for the Budapest Hills
aboard a train staffed by
13- to 17-year-olds – the narrow-gauge **Gyermekvasút**
(**Children's Railway**), which
will take you 12km (8 miles)
into the hills from the summit of Széchenyi-hegy. You
can hike into the woods
from stations en route – the
fourth stop, János-hegy, is
the highest point in and
around Budapest at 527m
(1729ft). A separate cog-
wheel railway takes you to
Széchenyi-hegy from its
lower station near the circular tower of the Budapest
Hotel, itself just a short walk
from Moszkva tér.

Below: *Pastel-shaded
houses line the streets of
Buda's Castle District.*

THE CASTLE DISTRICT

Fisherman's Bastion, the Matthias Church and King
Stephen statue are reflected in the copper-coloured glass
windows of Béla Pintér's **Budapest Hilton** Hotel, built in
1976 and incorporating the remains of a medieval
Dominican church and 17th-century Jesuit college.

The 14m (46ft) monument before the Matthias
Church, on the highest point of Castle Hill, is the **Holy
Trinity Column**, built in 1710–13 by grateful citizens to
mark the end of a plague. The column stands in the
midst of Szentháromság tér, where you will also find the
House of Hungarian Wines, occupying the cellars of the
one-time Finance Ministry building.

Streets of the Várnegyed (Castle District) spread
northwest of here towards the **Vienna Gate**, the four
arteries tightly packed with elegant pastel-coloured resi-
dences concealing fine courtyards, interspersed with the
occasional museum or restaurant.

The Hilton fronts Hess Andras tér, with its statue of
Pope Innocent XI. At No. 3, one of the district's oldest
houses dating from the late 14th century, the small red
hedgehog relief above the doorway symbolizes a former
owner; the building has also been used as an inn.

At Fortuna utca 4, the **Hungarian Museum of Commerce and Catering** takes a peep into past times of Budapest's hospitality industry, with century-old exhibits from prominent hotels, restaurants, cafés and places of entertainment.

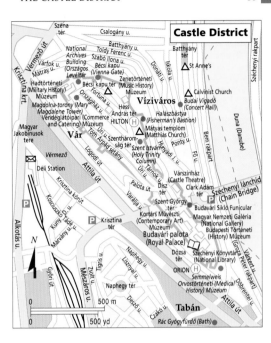

The **Music History Museum**, in the mid-18th-century Baroque **Erdödy Palace** at Táncsics Mihály utca 7, contains 18th- and 19th-century instruments, manuscripts, medals and paintings with a musical theme. An exhibition is devoted to the illustrious musical career of the great Hungarian composer **Béla Bartók**, who had a workshop here.

The **Medieval Jewish Prayer House** at No. 26 in the same street has artefacts relating to Jewish life in Buda; more comprehensive documentation of Budapest's Jewish community can be found in the **Jewish Museum** at Dohány utca 2 in Pest (*see* page 63).

Fortuna utca and Táncsics Mihály utca converge at the Lutheran Church close to the **Vienna Gate**, a reconstruction of an earlier entrance through the city walls with steps up each side and seats on top; it dates only from 1936, the 250th anniversary of the recapture of Buda from the Turks. Next to the gate is the massive stone-fronted **National Archives** building with its colourful diamond-patterned tiled roof complementing that of the Matthias Church.

Past the National Archives, the isolated brick structure reflected in the mirror glass of a modern office building is the **Mary Magdalene Tower** on Kapisztrán

CAVING ON HIGH

You can go caving in the northern Buda Hills – on organized tours through spectacular stalactite caves. The Pálvölgy cave system (Szépvölgyi út 162), Hungary's third largest, is noted for its stalactites and bat colony. The Szemlő hegy caves (Pusztaszeri út 35) have stalactites, stalagmites and crystal formations that look like bunches of grapes. The caves are about a kilometre apart and can be reached by taking the HÉV train from Batthyány tér to Szépvölgyi út and then bus 65.

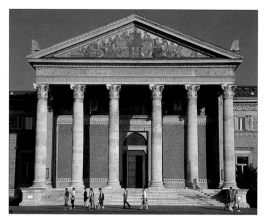

Above: *The neo-Classical lines of the Palace of Arts on Heroes' Square.*
Opposite: *The Castle Theatre (Várszínház) was formerly a church.*

tér, all that is left standing of a church once used by residents that was destroyed in World War II. A **carillon** of two dozen small bells on the exterior of the tower can be heard playing Hungarian folk tunes and other medleys; inside there is a small private **art gallery**.

Across the square from the tower is the **Military History Museum**, with a vast collection of all things military. It is housed in a former barracks stretching alongside the tree- and cannon-lined promenade of Tóth Árpád sétány facing the Buda Hills; the entrance is on the promenade. The museum contains a library, archives and map room, and frequently mounts exhibitions.

At the end of the promenade, beyond a flagpole striped in Hungary's national colours, is the flower-bedecked **grave of Abdurrahman**, the last Turkish ruler of Budapest, who was killed in 1686. The inscription refers to him as a 'valiant foe'.

Back on the square, the **statue** you will see is of **Friar John Kapisztrán** with a vanquished Turk – he inspired the Hungarians to victory over the Turks in the siege of Belgrade in 1456.

TOWARDS THE PALACE

From Kapisztrán tér, Úri utca leads you back the length of Castle District towards the Royal Palace; at No. 49 is the **Telephone Museum** in a wing of the **Klarisza Cloister**, reached through shady gardens. Many houses in the street offer glimpses of part-hidden courtyards, often with bench seats flanking their entrances.

At Úri utca 9 you are invited into the bowels of the earth, to tour the **Labyrinth of Buda Castle**. This takes you through a network of 1200m (1300yd) of natural caves and man-made passages, vaults and halls some 16m (52ft) down that were used as an air-raid shelter in World War II.

Úri utca and Tárnok utca join up at cobbled Dísz tér under the eye of a watchful **Hussar statue**. The war-damaged edifice situated here is the one-time **Ministry of Defence** building, derelict and in a state of advanced disrepair. Skirt its left side down Színház utca in the direction of the Royal Palace at the southern end of Castle Hill and you pass on your left the Baroque, yellow-fronted **Várszínház** (**Castle Theatre**), which was a Carmelite church until Joseph II dissolved the order in 1784. A few years later, the first play in Hungarian was performed here.

Next door is the **Sándor Palace**, dating from the early 19th century. Formerly the prime minister's residence, it is currently undergoing restoration, its future use undetermined. The top station of the Budavári Sikló funicular railway is a few paces further on. Across the expanse of Szent György tér before the Royal Palace gates, extensive excavations are taking place under the guidance of the Budapest History Museum.

The steps down to the broad terrace of the Royal Palace – like the Matthias Church an architectural blend of partly old and mainly recent – lead you past the giant bronze-sculpted *turul* (*see* panel, page 38). From here you enjoy fine unobstructed views across the river to the Pest side.

> **TREATMENTS FOR ALL**
>
> From the Holy Trinity Column by the Matthias Church, Tárnok utca heads towards the Royal Castle; located at No. 18 is the **Golden Eagle Pharmacy Museum**, in a building that dates from 1490. Founded in 1750, the pharmacy operated until 1913. Fascinating exhibits include ceramics, utensils, jars of antidotes, 2000-year-old 'mummy-head' powder for treating epilepsy, and an 18th-century distillation plant that the pharmacist also used for making brandy.

THE TURUL

The menacing bronze bird of prey, its talons grasping a sword, sitting above a gateway to the Royal Palace is the *turul*. The mythological bird is said to have made the grandmother of Prince Árpád pregnant, thus siring the early generations of Hungarian kings and earning its place in Hungarian history. It was adopted by the Hungarians as a **unifying symbol** against the Austrians and in recent years has become associated with far-right political elements.

Opposite: *One of the totemic animals known to Hungarians as the* turul.
Below: *The Royal Palace houses a museum and art gallery complex.*

The Royal Palace ★★★

The Royal Palace has its origins in medieval times. The first castle on the site was built by **Béla IV** around 1255 following the Mongol invasion; the Renaissance palace of **Matthias Corvinus** (1458–90) was one of the best until its destruction during the siege that ended the Turkish occupation in 1686.

The **Habsburgs** redeveloped the site, expanding their version of the palace through the 19th century, though it was never inhabited by them. The Royal Palace became **Admiral Horthy's** headquarters until he was forced out by the Nazis in 1944; in the subsequent Red Army siege of Buda, the **Nazis** made their last stand in the palace, which was left in ruins.

The Royal Palace you see today, complete with added dome, mostly dates from the 1950s and has a **museum and art gallery complex**. Within are the Museum of Contemporary Art (Ludwig Museum), the Hungarian National Gallery, the Budapest History Museum (Castle Museum), and the National Széchenyi Library.

The **Magyar Nemzeti Galéria (Hungarian National Gallery**, wings B, C and D) contains Hungarian pieces from the Middle Ages to the present time – an over-

whelming collection incorporating a medieval and Renaissance lapidarium, Gothic altarpieces, sculptures and panel paintings, along with canvases of leading Hungarian artists.

Some of the big names whose work is exhibited include **Mihály Munkácsy, László Paál, Gyula Benczúr**, the Impressionist **Pál Merse Szinyei**, the noted portrait painter **József Rippl-Rónai**, and renowned landscape artist **Tivadar Csontváry**, whose work drew posthumous praise from Picasso (*see* panels, this page and page 40).

By way of contrast, the **Kortárs Müvészti Múzeum (Museum of Contemporary Art**, wing A), set up in 1996 with a bequest from German industrialist Peter Ludwig, offers creations of pop artists such as **Warhol**,

Lichtenstein and **Hockney** alongside other work of the late 1980s and 1990s, much of it Hungarian. From the late 1970s, the wing contained the Museum of the Working Class Movement – hence the over-abundance of red marble walls.

At the far end of Lion Courtyard (the work of János Fadrusz in 1904), the **Budapesti Történeti Múzeum (Budapest History Museum**, wing E) traces 2000 years of Hungary's capital on three floors and features restored palace rooms from the 15th century. The **Gothic Hall** and **Crypt** contain prized statues of courtiers and religious figures discovered during excavations in 1974 – they are believed to have been discarded during 15th-century rebuilding work.

The **Országos Széchenyi Könyvtár (National Széchenyi Library**) also has its entrance in Lion Courtyard. Since 1802 it has accumulated more than two million **books** and countless **newspapers, manuscripts** and **musical scores**; a copy of every Hungarian-language publication from anywhere in the world finds its way here.

TIVADAR CSONTVÁRY

Kosztka Tivadar Csontváry (1853–1919) began his working life as a pharmacist and did not start painting until he was 41. He produced huge canvases of landscape scenes in Hungary, Italy, Dalmatia, Lebanon and Syria – among them *Ruins of the Greek Theatre at Taormina* and *Look Down on the Red Sea* – achieving greater recognition in the latter half of the 20th century than during his lifetime. Picasso's famous tribute to Csontváry was: 'And I thought that I was the only great painter of this century.' Much of his work is now displayed in the Csontváry Museum in Pécs.

Above: *The Budai Vigadó concert hall, now home to the Hungarian State Folk Ensemble.*
Opposite: *The Calvinist Church in Watertown.*

By the gateway into Lion Courtyard, guarded on each side by Fadrusz's pair of menacing lions, the **Matthias Well** with its bronze figures tells the story of the peasant girl **Szép Ilonka** (Fair Helen), who fell in love with King Matthias while he was out hunting. On discovering his identity and realizing her hopes were in vain, she died of a broken heart. The fountain was created by **Alajos Stróbl** in 1904.

From the Royal Palace, you can either retrace your steps to the funicular or leave from the rear of the Budapest History Museum towards the **Víziváros** (*see* below) or the **Tabán** (*see* page 42). The winding cobbled roadway descends through gateways beneath the heavily buttressed lower palace walls to the funicular's lower station on Clark Adám tér.

VÍZIVÁROS (WATERTOWN)

The cluster of streets between Castle Hill and the river, heading north from the lower station of the funicular, is the Víziváros (Watertown) – once a poor part of the city that was home to fishermen and craftsmen.

The station sits on Clark Adám tér, named after Scottish engineer Adam Clark, who masterminded the building of the adjacent **Chain Bridge** and the road tunnel beneath Castle Hill. In a small garden by the funicular, the **elliptical sculpture** serving no apparent purpose is in fact the 0-km stone, from which all distances in Hungary are measured.

The main artery of the Víziváros is **Fő utca**, a street of decaying apartment houses and tiny shops. Where it joins Corvin tér, new houses in the old style add colour to an essentially drab street.

On the south side of Corvin tér is the former **Capuchin Church**, bearing the raven and ring symbols of King Matthias Corvinus – the square is named after him. Across the square is the neo-Classical façade of the **Budai Vigadó** concert hall, which has certainly seen better days – it is now home to the **Hungarian State Folk Ensemble**, founded in 1951, which regularly performs in the building.

Between Fő utca and the river on Szilágyi Dezső tér, the brightly tiled roof belongs to the late 19th-century **Calvinist Church**. Moored close by is a **floating hotel** run by Koreans.

Fő utca opens out into Batthyány tér, city terminus of the **HÉV** suburban railway that heads north to the Danube-bend town of Szentendre. The yellow building 1m (3ft) below street level on the left, built in 1770, has a superb arched courtyard; it was formerly an inn where Casanova is said to have stayed and now houses the **Casanova Bar**.

Dominating the square is **St Anne's Parish Church** dating from 1740–62, with twin copper spires each sporting a clock. The interior is gloriously Baroque, with the ceiling artwork extra special. Two blocks further, on your left, is the former **Military Court of Justice** – an enormous brick building on Nagy Imre tér in which Nagy and other leaders of the 1956 Uprising were tried and executed two years later. A plaque refers to the 'martyrs of 28 October to 4 November 1956'.

Beyond, at Fő utca 84, is the distinctive **Király Gyógyfürdő** (Király thermal bath), with four small copper domes covering its octagonal pool. Decidedly Middle Eastern in appearance, it

> **BARTÓK TRIBUTE**
>
> The **Béla Bartók Museum** on the edge of the Buda Hills pays tribute to the Hungarian-born pianist and composer. The house at Csalán út 29 (bus route 29), where he lived from 1932 to 1940, contains a memorial room with original furniture and personal items – his folk art collection, letters and photos. The museum also contains a small exhibition of stamps, paintings and sculptures with Bartók as the theme. He was born in 1881 and emigrated to New York in the 1940s; he died there in 1945.

was first built by the Turks for their own garrison around 1580. Men and women may use the facilities on alternate days.

Crossing Ganz utca, you reach the bright yellow Baroque **St Flórián's Chapel**, built in 1759–60 as a hospital chapel with a donation from Buda's master baker Antal Christ. Owned since 1920 by the Greek Catholic Church, the building was raised a metre and a half in 1936–37 to protect it from the flooding Danube.

A **statue** of Polish general **József Bem**, who helped the Hungarians in the 1848–49 Independence War against the Habsburgs, occupies Bem tér. The statue has long been a rallying point for anti-government demonstrations; students gathered here at the start of the 1956 Uprising.

Left up Bem József utca is the **Foundry Museum**, housing smelting and casting equipment in an iron foundry built in 1858 that was in use until 1960.

THE TABÁN AND GELLÉRT HILL

The riverside area at the southern end of Castle Hill is known as the Tabán. At the foot of Castle Hill on its northern edge, the once ornate ballustraded walkways, columns and statues of the former **Castle Bazaar** have been derelict since the early 1980s. Across Ybl Miklós tér, the ornate **Castle Garden Kiosk** designed by Ybl is now a small **casino**.

Right: *The Király Bath brings a touch of the Orient to Budapest.*

Some of the prominent buildings in the Tabán are the **Semmelweis Museum of Medical History** at Apród utca 1–3 and the early 18th-century **Tabán Parish Church** on Szarvas tér. At the district's southern end are two Turkish-built bath houses, parts of which date from the 16th century – the yellow **Rác Fürdő** in the park, and **Rudas Fürdő** south of Elizabeth Bridge. A **statue** of the assassinated Queen Elizabeth ('Sissy') is situated at the bridge bearing her name (*see* panel, this page).

Climb the steps from the west side of Elizabeth Bridge up to Gellért Hill, continue right and you reach the **monument of St Gellért**, complete with colonnade, supposedly at the point where Hungarians unwilling to convert to Christianity hurled him to his death in 1046. There is conjecture over whether he was toppled in a barrow or a spiked barrel.

On the quiet tree-shrouded hill, the noise of the city rushes up to meet you. Steps and pathways lead upwards and after all that effort it's a bit of a letdown to find cars and coaches parked at the top beside the **Citadella** fortress, at an elevation of 230m (760ft). It's supremely worth the Fts 100 admission price for the magnificent **view** from the ramparts – on a clear day you can trace the course of the Danube right through the city.

The Citadella, which was built by the Habsburgs in 1854 but never called upon to defend the city, contains a

Above: *Gellért Hill offers grand views of the Hungarian capital.*

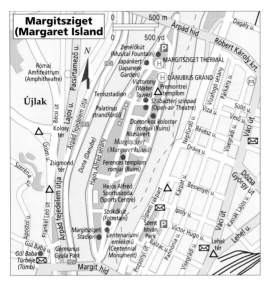

Margitsziget (Margaret Island)

Zenélőkút (Musical Fountain)
Japánkert (Japanese Garden)
MARGITSZIGET THERMAL
Római Amfiteátrum (Amphitheatre)
Víztorony (Water Tower)
DANUBIUS GRAND
Premontrei templom
Teniszstadion
Szabadtéri színpad (Open-air Theatre)
Palatinus strandfürdő
Domonkos kolostor romjai (Ruins)
Rózsakert
Kolosy tér
Margitsziget (Margaret Island)
Zsigmond tér
Ferences templom romjai (Ruins)
Hajós Alfréd Sportuszoda (Sports Centre)
Szökőkút (Fountain)
Margitszigeti Stadion
Szent István Park
Centenáriumi emlékmű (Centennial Monument)
Germanus Gyula Park
Gül Baba Türbéje (Tomb)
Margit híd
Árpád híd
Róbert Károly krt
Dagály u.
Újlak

Opposite: *The Gellért is the best-known of Budapest's spa hotels.*

THE STATUE PARK

Ever wondered what happened to the statues of Lenin, Russian soldiers and proletarian heroes that adorned Budapest's streets not so long ago? Take a bus to the **Szoborpark** (Statue Park) and you'll find out. In this open-air museum are statues that were removed during the Hungarian Uprising of 1956 and others that were toppled from their plinths after the fall of communism in 1989. The park is 10km (6 miles) southwest of the city centre; take the red-numbered bus 7–173 to Etele tér, then the yellow Volán bus towards Diósd.

small hotel, restaurant, beer terrace and a few cases of historical artefacts. The summit is crowned by Budapest's own **Statue of Liberty** – a 14m (45ft) lady holding the palm of freedom who once had Soviet soldiers grouped at her feet – designed in 1947 for Admiral Horthy by **Zsigmond Kisfaludi Stróbl**.

From the top it's a pleasing stroll down to the **Gellért Hotel**, grand old lady of Budapest hotels (*see* panel, this page) with its own splendid baths; on the way down, any children with you will have fun on the longest **playground slides** they are ever likely to experience.

MARGARET ISLAND

Wooded Margaret Island, just over 2km (1.5 miles) long, is the city's playground, a haven for strollers and joggers and a retreat from the traffic coursing its way along the river banks. Alight from tram No. 4 or 6 on **Margit híd** (**Margaret Bridge**) and you have a fine perspective of the city – alternatively, bus 26 will take you right on to the island from the western train station.

Heading north from Margaret Bridge, an extensive **sports centre** to your left offers tennis; there's a full-scale athletics stadium tucked behind the trees, beyond which you can hire a bike or four-wheel pedal carriage to explore the island. For the less energetic visitor, battery-operated cars can be rented by the hour or half-hour.

The pointed monument resembling a giant cracked-open seed pod on the roundabout ahead is the **Centennial Monument**, erected in 1973 to commemorate the centenary of the joining of Buda, Pest and Óbuda into the present-day capital city. It's one of the city's odder monuments; as well as the three shields, the inside contains cogwheels, helmets, knives and other miscellany.

The **National Swimming Pool** to your left was built in the 1930s by **Alfréd Hajós** (1878–1955), Hungarian winner of the 100m and 1200m swimming events at the first Olympiad in Athens in 1896. Two-thirds of the way along the island, the **Palatinus Strand** complex is another swimmers' idyll, with outdoor thermal pools, water slides and terraces for sunbathing.

With birdsong from the plane trees, the scent of freshly mown grass in the air and **wooded parkland** as far as the eye can see, it's hard to believe that you are in the centre of a bustling, modern city.

Two walls and a crumbling tower are all that remain of a 13th-century **Franciscan church**. Cut diagonally right across the park to reach another ruin – that of the former **Dominican church and convent**. A little way further on is an octagonal **water tower** (1911), with a café at its base flanking an open-air theatre; hereabouts, busts of several Hungarian worthies are dotted among the trees.

An unexpected gem is the tiny **St Michael's Premonstratensian Church**. Destroyed during the Turkish Wars in 1541, it was rebuilt in 1930–31; the 15th-century bell was discovered in the roots of a walnut tree uprooted by a storm in 1914.

At the north end of the island are the two large **spa hotels** of the Danubius Group – the Grand and the Thermal.

GRAND OLD LADY

The **Gellért**, which opened in 1918, is Budapest's grand old **hotel** – a world-famous Art Nouveau property that has hosted generations of celebrities down the years. The Gellért's main **thermal bath** is one of the wonders of Budapest, with its high columns, majolica tiles and lion water-spouts. It is entered on the right side of the hotel, on Kelenhegyi út. You will also find outdoor swimming and thermal pools here.

Below: *Meet the elegant umbrella ladies of Óbuda, an inspired creation by Imre Varga.*

AQUINCUM

A 20-minute ride on the HÉV suburban train from Batthyány tér station brings you to Aquincum – and what is left of the **Roman town** that was the provincial **capital of Lower Pannonia**, close to the Roman Empire's Danube frontier. You can identify the streets, forum, temples, public baths (one containing a mosaic of wrestlers), market hall, shops and houses of the Roman civilian town from the wall foundations. The **military base** with its 6000 soldiers was sited in Óbuda (Old Buda), around present-day Flórián tér, where only a few scattered remains are now visible.

Aquincum became the centre of Pannonia's commercial life and prospered in the 2nd and 3rd centuries. Sacked on several occasions in the 3rd and 4th centuries, it eventually fell to the Huns early in the 5th century.

The **museum**, in neo-Classical style, was built in 1894 and contains a variety of artefacts from the site, including a reconstructed water organ from the period. Across Szentendrei út is the **amphitheatre**, the Romans' cultural and leisure centre. This was Aquincum's venue for concerts, plays and sporting contests, attended by up to 4000 enthusiastic citizens at a time – it was also the scene of gladiator contests and animal fights. Next to the amphitheatre were the **gladiators' barracks**.

ÓBUDA

The heart of Óbuda – which all but lost its identity in 1873 when it was merged with the new Budapest – is a short walk from Árpád híd station on the HÉV suburban railway. Its centre is **Flórián tér**, bisected by the road off the bridge; here, next to the Corinthia Aquincum Hotel, are the yellow Baroque **Óbuda Parish Church** and former **Óbuda Synagogue**, now TV studios. A 10-minute walk northwest of Flórián tér, at Meggyfa utca 19–21, is the **Hercules Villa**, named after the 3rd-century floor mosaic of a former Roman villa.

Above Left: *Museum and wall foundations of the Roman Aquincum.*

North of Árpád híd is picturesque **Fő tér**, with its restored collection of Baroque houses and restaurants in a quaint village-like atmosphere. The former Zichy mansion on cobbled Szentlékek tér contains the **Vasarely Museum** (*see* panel, this page) and the **Kassák Museum**, with work from the early 20th century. The comprehensive **Zsigmond Kun Collection** of folk art occupies an 18th-century townhouse at Fő tér 4. Four unhappy ladies with bright shiny umbrellas wait beneath a lampost on Laktanya utca – the creation of **Imre Varga**, whose work is displayed further down the street in a gallery at No. 7.

One HÉV train stop to the south are the remains of the **Roman military amphitheatre** on Pacsirtamező utca; even larger than the Colisseum in Rome, it could hold 15,000 spectators.

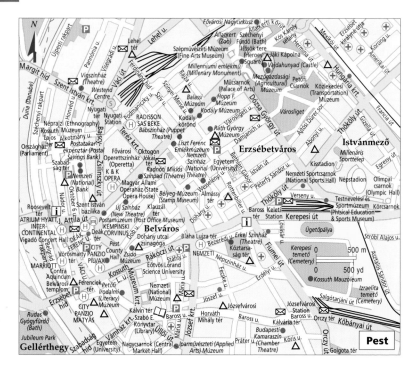

THE HEART OF PEST

Pest is the **commercial** heart of Budapest, its grand buildings dating largely from the late 19th century. Much of interest to the visitor will be found in the **V district**, between the Danube and the **Kiskörút** (**Little Ring Road**), to the southeast of the Chain Bridge. A second semicircular 'layer' is created between the Kiskörút and the **Nagykörút** (**Great Ring Road**), beyond which exploration leads you out to **Városliget**, the City Park.

Vörösmarty tér is the tourist heart of Pest, its leafy cobblestone expanse bounded by a mix of building styles. In its midst sits the poet **Mihály Vörösmarty** (1800–50); the statue's inscription, from his patriotic piece *Szósat (Appeal)*, reads 'Be faithful to your country forever, oh Hungarians'. The statue, in Italian marble, wears a protective covering each winter to save it from cracking.

At the foot of the elegant white façade on the north side is the famous **Gerbeaud coffee house**, its chairs and tables spilling onto the square in summer. The Swiss confectioner Emile Gerbeaud bought the patisserie in 1884 and turned it into a favoured venue of Budapest's coffee drinkers; the service now may be a little slower, but the pastries, among them the house speciality *konyakos meggy* (dark chocolate containing a cherry soaked in cognac), are delicious.

Less harmonious to the surrounds is the concrete and copper-glass front of the building on the west side housing the **Zeneszalon** music store and **Vigadó** ticket service – here you can buy tickets for any performance or happening in the city (a full programme of events is posted in the window).

> **LOOKOUT POINT**
>
> The best overview of Pest, from a height of 65m (213ft), can be obtained by climbing the 302 steps to the observation terrace at the top of **St Stephen's Basilica**. The 360-degree panorama is unrivalled on this side of the city. If you can manage only half that climb, a lift will take you to a point from where you ascend the final 137 spiral stairs. The lookout is open from 1 April to 31 October.

Shopping Hub ★★

Behind the outdoor **Café Vörösmarty** that all but seals off Deák Ferenc utca for half the year, the grand columned building is the **Bank Palace**, built in 1915 and now occupied by the **Budapest Stock Exchange**. Heading south off Vörösmarty tér is **Váci utca**, the capital's shopping hub. Marks and Spencer is here, along with boutiques and designer shops. If you're looking for souvenirs, the whole range is available – laceware, costumed dolls, hand-painted eggs and colourful embroidered children's dresses, napkins and tablecloths that make excellent gifts. Towards the end of the shops, on the right of the street at No. 33 near Elizabeth Bridge, is the **Jegyiroda** ticket service (*see* Budapest At a Glance, page 73), an entertainment booking agency.

Alternatively, soon after leaving Vörösmarty tér, take Kristóf tér on the left, with its appealing fisher girl statue, to **Szervita tér**, dominated by the 18th-century **Servite Church**. Note the fine gable mosaic depicting Hungaria

Below: *Gerbeaud coffee house is an institution not to be missed.*

opposite, above the Dr Jeans shop at No. 3; the contemporary looking **Rózsavölgyi building** at No. 5 dates from 1912, the inspiration of **Béla Lajtha**.

From Szervita tér, **Petőfi Sándor utca** – one of 17 streets and squares in Budapest named after Hungary's greatest poet – heads south a block east of Váci utca with more shops and the main post office at No. 13; traffic-free streets link the two shopping zones. Head west along Pilvax köz to the colourful square of **Kamermayer Károly tér**, with the green **Pest County Hall** and vast pink and gold 18th-century **City Hall**, stretching into the distance down Városház utca.

Károly Kamermayer (1829–97) was Budapest's first mayor. His **statue** adorns the square; the narrow streets leading off it contain small antique shops. Back on Petőfi Sándor utca, the dark and forbidding **Párizsi Udvar arcade** next to the Ferenciek tere underpass contains a real rarity – a **hologram shop**.

The **Franciscan Church** opposite, on the corner of Kossuth utca, is noted for its wall relief recounting

the heroics of **Baron Miklós Wesselényi**, who rescued many Budapest citizens in his boat during the great flood of 13–16 March 1838; despite his efforts, more than 400 died.

The yellow building on the left past the underpass is the **university library**; beyond the freshly modernized office building on Károlyi utca is the **Petőfi Irodalmi Múzeum** (**Petőfi Literature Museum**) in the 18th-century the **Károlyi Palace**, itself newly refurbished. It contains the works and possessions of **Sándor Petőfi** and other noted Hungarian authors.

The large Baroque church on the right is the **University Church** from the mid-18th century; a copy of

Poland's *Black Madonna of Czestochowa* hangs above the altar. The church stands next to the faculty building of **Eötvös Science University** on Egyetem tér; students crowd the benches around the square and the cafés of Kecskeméti utca.

On the right, Szerb utca leads towards Váci utca and contains the **Serbian Orthodox Church**; on the corner, a wall relief shows the extent of the flood of March 1838. The Mercure Korona Hotel is near the site of the **Kecskemét Gate**, part of the city's medieval defences.

Hungarian National Museum ★★★

A block north on Múzeum körút is the neo-Classical **Magyar Nemzeti Múzeum (Hungarian National Museum)**, the largest in Hungary. Designed by **Mihály Pollack**, it opened in 1847 and traces Hungarian history from the arrival of the Magyars to the present day. Its redevelopment is due to be completed in 2002, by which time the **crown jewels** will have been returned from Parliament, their home since the millennium celebration of King Stephen's coronation. A significant date in the museum's long history is 15 March 1848, when Petőfi delivered the words of the patriotic **National Song** from its steps – firing the revolution against the Habsburgs that led to the War of Independence.

Above: *The Chain Bridge leads across the Danube to the Royal Palace.*
Opposite: *The elegant interior of the Hungarian National Museum.*

RETAIL THERAPY

The **Közponi Vásárcsarnok (Great Market Hall)** on Vámház körút, on the Pest side of Szabadság híd (Liberty Bridge), was one of five similarly styled indoor market buildings constructed in the late 19th century. The hall is on three levels – you enter by the middle one, packed with meats and vegetables. Head downstairs for fish – there are tanks of live creatures at the back – and up to the gallery with its profusion of lacework, embroidery and other souvenir items. The **Fakana restaurant** on the gallery will feed you cheaply and well.

Above: *The Marriott is one of several deluxe hotels along the Danube.*

ALONG THE DANUBE

However you intend to fill your time in Budapest, leave an hour or two free to wander at leisure beside the Danube. Blue it isn't, but the views across the river to Gellért Hill, the Royal Palace and over the **Széchenyi lánchíd (Széchenyi Chain Bridge)** to the Castle District are exceptional. Tram No. 2 on the Pest side partly covers the same journey, but walking allows time to stop and gaze.

The **Duna-korzó (Danube Promenade)** begins on busy **Roosevelt tér**, where traffic crossing the Chain Bridge spills off in all directions. Facing the square is the Art Nouveau **Gresham Palace**, in a state of advanced decay at the time of writing but due to metamorphose into the deluxe **Four Seasons Hotel**. The splendid façade of the building, put up in 1904 to house an insurance company, is to be retained. It will be in complete contrast to the **Atrium Hyatt** and **Inter-Continental**, two other river-facing luxury hotels created in the early 1980s. Swanky **restaurant boats** tied up along the Promenade near the Inter-Continental do brisk business on sunny days and balmy summer evenings – claim your table by the river and splash out some forints on a Hungarian feast.

Across leafy Vigadó tér, sporting a new fountain and trimmed with lace stalls, is the arcaded **Pesti Vigadó** concert hall. The Vigadó, one of Budapest's premier cultural venues, was completed in 1865 to the design of **Frigyes Feszl** and restored to its original Romantic style after World War II; it was reopened in 1980. Improved acoustically since the rebuilding, the Vigadó seats 640 in its Great Hall. Close by is one of Budapest's less attractive sights – the massive windowless back wall of the river-fronting deluxe **Marriott Hotel**, built in 1969.

Further towards the gleaming white **Erzsébet híd (Elizabeth Bridge)**, the Orthodox church through the trees on Petőfi tér is from the 1870s; in gardens by the

POET AND PATRIOT

Sándor Petőfi, who lived a short life between 1823 and 1849, was Hungary's greatest poet – compared with Robert Burns and studied by Hungarian children, yet relatively unknown outside his home country. His statue in Petőfi tér, at the Pest end of Elizabeth Bridge, is by Miklós Izso and Adolf Huszar. Erected in 1882, it shows Petőfi reciting his patriotic anthem *'Talpre, Magyar'* ('Rise up, Hungarians') that sparked the **1848 War of Independence** against the Habsburgs. The patriotic young poet died at the age of 26 in battle.

Promenade, the **statue of Sándor Petőfi** (*see* panel, opposite) is traditionally a rallying point for demonstrations.

The twin spires right by the flyover leading off
Elizabeth Bridge belong to the **Inner City Parish Church**,
Pest's oldest church – there has been a church on this site
since the 12th century. Close to the church on **Március 15
tér** are the excavated remnants of a **Roman fort** known
as **Contra Aquincum**, an outpost of the garrison in
Óbuda. The name of the square (15 March) marks the
start of the anti-Habsburg revolution in 1848.

Beyond Elizabeth Bridge, the Duna-korzó takes over
the **Belgrád rakpart**, a focus of conflict between the Red
Army and the Nazis in the last days of World War II.

St Stephen's Basilica ★★

Your travels in Pest will no doubt make you familiar with
Deák Ferenc tér – it's where the three Metro lines intercon-
nect, the site of the bus station and a major tram stop – you
will also find the **Underground Railway Museum** here.
From the square, commonly abbreviated like most 'full
name' streets and squares to simply Deák tér, the dome of
St Stephen's Basilica, Budapest's **cathedral**, appears above
the bus station – hopefully the lengthy restoration, that has
required much of the building to be scaffolded,
will soon be complete. Restoration has also been
taking place on the interior, with its abundance of
marble, gilding and frescoes.

Work on the Basilica started under **József
Hild** in 1851, but was not completed for another
54 years – in no small way because the dome collapsed during a storm in January 1868. With
fresh plans drawn up by **Miklós Ybl**, designer of
the Hungarian State Opera House, the building
was begun again almost from scratch and, following Ybl's death in 1891, completed by **József
Kauser** in 1905.

In a gold casket before **Our Lady's Altar** is
the mummified right **hand of St Stephen**,
Hungary's most venerated possession. It found
its way to Budapest in 1771, having been kept in

Below: *Traffic swarms
over the Elisabeth Bridge
onto the Buda side.*

Transylvania, Ragusa (the present Dubrovnik) and Vienna; spirited away to the West in 1944 during World War II, it was returned after the war. The **Panorama Tower** gives an excellent overview of Pest; the **Treasury** contains some prized artefacts.

The Hungarian State Opera House ***

The straight and grand boulevard of **Andrássy út** (at one time Stalin Avenue) heads northeast from Deák tér, and five minutes' walk past the **Post Office Museum** on your right brings you before the neo-Renaissance **Magyar Állami Operaház (Hungarian State Opera House)**, built in 1884. It looks good on the outside – and it's even better within, all gilded and marble-clad with fine frecoes, the creation of Miklós Ybl, and containing the output of leading 19th-century Hungarian painters. It seats around 1300 concert-goers. **Statues** of composers **Ferenc Erkel**, the writer of Hungary's national anthem, and **Franz Liszt** flank the main entrance. If you can't make a performance, take an afternoon tour, for which tickets can be bought at an office situated to the right of the building.

From the same period, the **Hungarian Dance Academy** directly opposite is the creation of leading Art Nouveau builder **Ödön Lechner** and strikes a nice balance across Andrássy út. To the rear of the Academy, the **Új Színház (New Theatre)** at Paulay Ede utca 35 is a steely-grey Art Deco building adorned with monkeys above the doorway and gold and blue decoration aloft.

The **Művész Kávéhaz** at Andrássy út 29 (open until midnight) is one of Budapest's best-known coffee houses. It has been here since 1898 and delivers coffee, cake and apple strudel in the finest tradition. Beyond, the cross-street of **Nagymező utca** is Budapest's **theatre-land**, with a number of theatres and some non-touristy coffee bars. Just to your right are the **Budapesti Kamaraszínház** (the **Budapest Chamber Theatre**) and the **Miklós Radnóti Theatre**; to your left the restored **Budapesti Operett Színház** (**Budapest Operetta**) and **Thália Theatre**. Sheltered beneath

a mirrored canopy, wedge-shaped paving stones tell the Thália's history from its opening as the Jardin d'Hiver (winter garden) in 1913. With its theatres, smattering of late bars, clubs and a casino, the street has been tagged 'Broadway', but don't expect too much – the resemblance is minimal.

The **Párizsi Nagyáruház** building, at Andrássy út 39, contains a department store; the original opened in 1911. Past the green swathe of Jókai tér and Liszt Ferenc tér, you meet the eight-sided **Oktogon** intersection with the inner ring road known as **Nagykörút** – a name you won't find on the map. Across Oktogon, Andrássy út continues for another 1.5km (1 mile) to **Hősök tere**. On the left, pause outside No. 60, the building with the plaques – as the headquarters of the feared secret police during and post-World War II, it was once Budapest's most hated building.

Opposite, on the corner of Vörösmarty utca, is the **Ferenc Liszt Memorial Museum**, in his former apartment of the Academy of Music he established. Liszt lived here from 1881 until his death five years later. Most of the furniture is original; rare musical instruments displayed include Liszt's travelling keyboard and glass piano. There

Above: *Stylish exterior of the State Opera House.*
Opposite: *St Stephen's Basilica, completed in 1905, took 54 years to build.*

STAMPS AND COINS

Pest caters for philatelists and numismatists in two specialist collections – the small **Bélyegmúzeum** (**Stamp Museum**) at Harsfa utca 47, and the **Banknote and Coin Collection** at the Magyar Nemzeti Bank at Szabadság tér 8. The latter is an exhibition of Hungarian coins and banknotes down the ages, from a **denarius** of King Stephen I – Hungary's oldest coin – to banknotes showing millions of **forints** from the postwar period of massive inflation; there is a section on Transylvanian currency.

Above: *Writers and artists made the Café New York their second home.*

are also personal effects and manuscripts. Next to it is the **Budapesti Bábszínház** (**Budapest Puppet Theatre**).

Continue along Andrássy út for a glimpse into the life of another leading Hungarian composer – that of **Zoltán Kodály** (1882–1967), in the **Kodály Memorial Museum** at No. 1 Kodály körönd. The rooms in the neo-Renaissance mansion, one of four faded blocks surrounding the square, are much as they were when Kodály lived there, with pictures, manuscripts and other documents.

The **György Ráth Museum**, at Városligeti fasor 12 (turn right down Bajza utca), and **Museum of Eastern Asiatic Arts**, at Andrássy út 103, share a superb collection of Asian artefacts assembled by businessman Ferenc Hopp on forays to the Far East. Hereabouts, many of the huge villas are now embassies or company headquarters – or have been divided up into highly prestigious apartments.

Heroes' Square ★★

The vast expanse of **Hősök tere** (**Heroes' Square**), with its neo-Classical museum and exhibition buildings flanking the **Millenary Monument** and **colonnade**, leaves a lasting impression. The square was created in 1896 to commemorate the 1000th anniversary of the Magyars' arrival in the Carpathian Basin. Atop the 36m (118ft) column is the **Archangel Gabriel**, who is said to have appeared in a dream to Stephen and offered him the Hungarian crown; at the base of the column are chieftains of the **seven original Magyar tribes**. The colonnade of two semicircles carries **statues** of leading Hungarian rulers, from King Stephen down the centuries. In front is the **Tomb of the Unknown Soldier**.

The larger of the two imposing neo-Classical buildings is the **Szépmüvészeti Múzeum** (**Museum of Fine Arts**), completed in 1906 and housing the nation's leading international collection. Works include giant canvases by **Krafft** (*The Crowning of Emperor Francis*) and **Piloty** (*Nero on the Burnt Ruins of Rome*). Upstairs, an interesting Spanish collection includes *Penitent Magdalene* by **El Greco** and *Peasants at Table* by **Velázquez**. The 19th-century collection contains pieces by **Gauguin**, **Monet**, **Renoir** and **Delacroix**; there are also extensive Italian, Dutch and Flemish assemblies and a limited British representation featuring works by **Reynolds**, **Gainsborough**, **Hoppner** and **Constable**.

Across the square, the **Mücsarnok** (**Palace of Arts**) is Hungary's biggest exhibition hall, with large rooms for staging short-term exhibitions. The six-lane cobbled avenue to the right facing the Palace of Arts, Dózsa György út, was Hungary's version of Red Square, where communist leaders carried out military reviews under the watchful eye of **Lenin** – the statue is now in the **Statue Park** (*see* panel, page 45).

The **Palace of Wonders Interactive Scientific Playhouse** provides a hands-on environment that makes science fun for youngsters up to 16 years. Weird and wonderful exhibits and activities keep the kids entertained at Váci út 19 (to the left of the Western Station in Pest). The **Budapest Puppet Theatre**, at Andrássy út 69, has classic fairytales on offer, though unfortunately only in Hungarian. The **Vidámpark** amusement park, **Municipal Circus** and **Zoo**, all located in the Városliget (City Park), all have their young fans.

Left: *The Tomb of the Unknown Soldier in Heroes' Square.*

SPORTING SCENE

Budapest's large sporting centre, situated roughly mid-way between the Városliget (City Park) and Kerepesi Cemetery, is focused on the **Népstadion**, a 76,000-seat stadium that stages inter-national football matches and rock concerts. Other venues on the site include the **Kisstadion**, the indoor **Budapest Sportcsarnok** and **Olimpiaicsarnok**. The **FTC Stadium** of leading Budapest soccer club Ferencváros is at Üllői út 129, opposite the Népliget (People's Park) on the main highway that leads south-east to the airport – the club's distinctive green and white colours are evident throughout Ferencváros, an inner-city suburb.

INTO THE PARK

Hősök tere is on the edge of the green and inviting **Városliget (City Park)**, which like the square was laid out for the 1896 millenary celebrations. It's Budapest's largest park, a square kilometre in size, offering plenty to do for all ages; the park has its own castle, a boating lake that becomes a skating rink in winter, circus, zoo, amusement park, grand bathhouse – and a couple of museums for good measure.

First there is the **castle**, which was completed in 1904. You will pick out **Vajdahunyad vára** to the right of Kós Károly sétány, the main road into the park that bridges the boating lake. Modelled on the Transylvanian castle of Hunyadi, it is a mix of contrasting Gothic, Renaissance and Romanesque styles that somehow blend to create a fairytale impression. Within its walls are the **Hungarian Agricultural Museum** – the largest agricultural museum in Europe. The **Chapel of Ják**, part-modelled on the small chapel at Ják in western Hungary, is opposite.

By the castle you'll find one of Budapest's favourite statues – that of Anonymous, the unknown medieval

Left: *Széchenyi Fürdő is one of Europe's largest public baths.*
Opposite: *Vajdahunyad, Budapest's own city castle, is surrounded by a moat.*

chronicler ascribed to King Béla, but which King Béla no-one is sure. The writings of this figure – hooded for anonymity – have provided much of what is known about medieval Hungary.

To the south of the castle across the boating lake is a statue of **George Washington**, erected in 1906 and funded by some of the estimated three million Austro-Hungarians who emigrated to the United States between the 1870s and World War I. East of the castle, on the edge of the park, the **Transportation Museum** contains model railway locomotives and early cars; the museum's space section is housed close by in the **Petőfi Hall**, a rock and pop music venue.

Across Kós Károly sétány, the road cutting through the park, the palatial **Széchenyi Fürdő** (1913) – one of Europe's largest public baths – is clearly identified by its series of copper domes. There are indoor and out-door thermal baths, with mud treatments, jet massage and the whole range of spa experiences available. The temperature of the pools varies from 27°C to 38°C – you can even play chess as you bathe, using a floating cork board.

Beyond the baths are the zoo, circus and amusement park all in a row across Állatkerti körút. The **Municipal Circus** is directly opposite the baths, with thrice-daily performances (but not Monday or Tuesday). To its right

---

UPSCALE DINING

Gundel, next door to the Zoo, is Hungary's best-known restaurant, where the accent is very much on traditional Hungarian recipes. It was founded by Károly Gundel in 1894 and is known both for its excellent cuisine and the oil paintings adorning the walls of its colonnaded interior (for key to the artists, see the back of the menu). A favourite on the menu is the *palacsinta* (Gundel pancake), a crêpe filled with flambéed chocolate sauce and crushed walnuts. After dinner to the accompaniment of a gypsy ensemble, diners may be invited to look over the extensive wine cellar.

Above: *The 19th-century Központi Vásárcsarnok (Great Market Hall) near Liberty Bridge.*

is the **Vidámpark**, an amusement park that has seen better days but has some good old-fashioned rides – a wooden roller-coaster, wooden carousel and Ferris wheel among them – plus a Looping Star and the stomach-churning Ikarus. There are long-term plans for the amusement park to be resited, which would allow the **City Zoo** much-needed expansion. The zoo lies behind an imposing entrance south of the circus and is known as much for its early 20th-century Art Nouveau buildings – they include the Elephant House, Palm House and Bird House – as for its inmates. The zoo includes a **botanical garden**.

NORTH OF DEÁK TÉR

A few blocks north of Deák tér is the leafy expanse of **Szabadság tér (Independence Square)**, one of Budapest's largest squares, which was laid out in 1897 on the site of a huge former barracks. It was in these barracks that **Count Lajos Batthyány**, prime minister of the independent Hungarian government, was shot after the Habsburgs had crushed the Hungarian insurrection in October 1849 – the spot has been marked since 1926 by an eternal flame.

On the square's southeast corner is the Hungarian **National Bank (MNB) building**, its façade adorned with reliefs depicting work, work … and more work. The Art Nouveau block next door is the **US Embassy**, where Cardinal Mindszenty took refuge from 1956 until 1971; the **statue** on the green before it is of **Harry Hill Bandholtz**, an army general from the US peace-keeping force who prevented Romanians from looting the Hungarian National Museum in 1919.

WEST AND EAST

Pest's two great **railway stations**, the Nyugati (Western) and Keleti (Eastern), lie 3km (2 miles) apart. The Western station, facing Nyugati tér, was completed in 1877 by the **Eiffel Company** of Paris. It's a huge, cavernous structure of iron and glass covering 25,000m² (29,900 sq yd) that has rightly become a subject of conservation – in the early 1970s a train crashed right through the glass panel and came to rest by the tram stop outside. **Keleti**, Pest's other major railway edifice facing Baross tér, was built in 1884 and renovated in the 1980s.

Behind the embassy on Hold utca, half the block is taken up by Ödön Lechner's decorated Art Nouveau former **Post Office Savings Bank**. Note the bees ascending to the roof – it could have been Gaudí-inspired. Across Hold utca is a large indoor market hall from 1896.

At the north end of the square is the **Soviet Army memorial**, a rare reminder of 'Big Brother' still standing in the capital. Occupying the entire west side of Szabadság tér is the headquarters of **Hungarian Television (MTV)**, in the former **Stock Exchange** built in the early 1900s – note the twin towers in the style of an eastern temple.

Another block northwest and you are on Kossuth tér gazing at the **Hungarian Parliament building**, having just passed an unusual **statue** of a man on a footbridge on **Vértanuk tere (Martyrs' Square)**. The man is **Imre Nagy**, the former prime minister who was tried and executed in 1958 after the uprising two years earlier; the controversial statue, by **Tamás Varga**, was erected in 1996 on the centenary of his birth. **Statues** of Hungarian heroes **Lajos Kossuth**, the 1848 Revolution leader, and **Prince Ferenc Rákóczi II**, who united Hungarians against the Habsburgs, are situated at opposite ends of Kossuth tér.

STAR COMPOSER

Franz (Ferenc) Liszt (1811–86) is remembered as Hungary's leading Romantic composer; also as pianist and founder of the **Academy of Music** in the Budapest house in which he lived from 1881 until his death (Vörösmarty utca 35, now the **Liszt Museum**). Liszt did not settle in Budapest until 1875, after spells in Paris, Weimar and Rome. His output was prodigious. In 1856, his *Esztergom Mass* was chosen to be performed for the consecration of the new **Esztergom Basilica**. In 1867, he composed the *Coronation Mass* for the crowning of Emperor **Franz Joseph I** as king of Hungary.

Below: *Budapest's Parliament building was styled on the Palace of Westminster in London.*

Opposite: *The Holocaust Memorial in Budapest's Jewish district recalls the persecution of the city's Jews.*

Parliament Building ✦✦✦

The riverside Parliament building, styled by **Imre Steindl** on London's Palace of Westminster, was completed in 1902, having been 17 years in the making. This grand neo-Gothic edifice, with its 691 rooms and 18 courtyards, stretches 268m (293yd) along the Danube; its cupola is 96m (315ft) high, marking the date of the Magyars' conquest of Hungary in 896. Sadly, the building was faced with porous limestone, necessitating renovation work that continues to this day. There are daily tours of the building in English at 10:00 and 14:00.

The two large buildings facing Parliament across Kossuth tér are the **Ministry of Agriculture** on the right and **Ethnography Museum** on the left. The neo-Renaissance museum was built in 1896 as the **Supreme Court**; it now houses a permanant exhibition, Folk Culture of the Hungarians, a highlight of which is the display of costumes from the late 19th and early 20th centuries.

Following the east bank of the Danube beyond the Parliament building brings you to **Margit híd** (**Margaret Bridge**), providing access to Margaret Island (see page 44). The road off the bridge, Szent István körút (part of the outer ring road known as Nagykörút) brings you shortly to Budapest's Western station by Nyugati tér. To its left is the **Westend Centre**, one of Europe's biggest shopping complexes, full of familiar and less familiar names. The site includes the new upmarket **Hilton Westend Hotel**.

THE JEWISH DISTRICT

The **VII district** east of Deák tér – known as **Erzsébetváros**, or Elizabeth Town – has retained some of its prewar atmosphere, when it was the centre of Budapest's Jewish community. Amble through the streets around Klauzál tér and you will stumble upon synagogues and shops still at the heart of Jewish life, survivors from 1944–45 when 70,000 Jewish people were walled up inside the ghetto.

The **Great Synagogue**, at Dohány utca 2–8, is the world's largest outside New York and can hold up to 3000 worshippers. It was completed in 1859 in Oriental-

Byzantine style with patterned brickwork inspired by ancient Middle Eastern ruins. Extensive renovation work carried out in the 1990s was part-funded by a New York-based charity headed by the actor Tony Curtis, whose parents were Hungarian emigrants in the 1920s. The **Jewish Museum** on the site was the birthplace of **Theodor Hertzl** (1860–1904), the father of modern Zionism.

The poignant **Holocaust Memorial** in adjacent Wesselényi utca takes the form of a metal tree, its leaves bearing the names of Hungarian Jewish families. Close by is a **monument to Carl Lutz**, a Swiss consul who supplied Jewish people with false wartime papers; the **Raoul Wallenberg Memorial Garden** is named after the Swedish diplomat who helped Jews to escape the Nazi clutches (*see* panel, opposite). There are several other synagogues in the area – they include the Art Nouveau **Orthodox Synagogue** at Kazinczy utca 29–31, the **Moorish Conservative Synagogue** dating from 1872 at Rumbach Sebestyén utca 11 and the **Small Synagogue**, dating from 1364, at Táncsics Mihály utca 26.

PLACE OF REST

The expansive **Kerepesi Cemetery**, a short walk from Eastern railway station, is the final resting place of many prominent Hungarians. Pick up a map at the entrance on Fiumei út and find your way along paths among the splendid mausoleums and simple graves. Those interred here include former communist leader **János Kádár**; national heroes **Lajos Kossuth**, **Lajos Batthyány** and **Ferenc Deák**; the 'Nightingale of the Nation', **Lujza Blaha**; and the poet **Endre Ady**. Buried in a single large plot are many who lost their lives in the **1956 Uprising**.

Budapest at a Glance

BEST TIMES TO VISIT

Budapest boasts upwards of 2000 hours of sunshine annually, a figure that effectively stretches its tourist season from early spring until autumn. Though high summer is the best time to soak up that sunshine in the resorts of Lake Balaton, on the Great Plain and in the northern uplands, Hungary's capital – like cities the world over – is at its best just out of the high season. Late June and September/October are the best times to enjoy Budapest – after the showers of April and May and before the wettest month, which is November. However, if you choose July or August, the Danube and nearby Buda Hills can provide welcome relief if it gets too hot and humid for comfort. The wooded hills are especially attractive in autumn, when the leaves change colour. Don't be put off from visiting Budapest in winter – though the winter temperatures can be pretty cold, the winter months are the driest of the year. There is usually little snowfall and Budapest offers a very good spread of museums and coffee houses in which to thaw out.

GETTING THERE

By air: International flights into Hungary arrive at Budapest's newly expanded Ferihegy International Airport. National carrier Malév Hungarian Airlines and British Airways operate at least one flight daily from London Heathrow; Malév also flies daily from London Gatwick and Manchester. There are air connections from most major European cities, and Malév also flies from New York and Toronto.

From the airport, you can take a taxi (expensive), airport minibus or airport shuttle bus. The Airport Minibus Service (tel: 296 8555/8993/6283, Fts 1200 one way) delivers you conveniently to your city address; you can buy a return ticket in the airport arrival hall, and in any case you must book your return 24 hours in advance. The Airport Centrum Minibus shuttle service (Fts 600) links the airport with Erzsébet tér in central Pest in the hours between 05:30 and 21:30. A public transport alternative is to take the bus with the red number 93 (the black 93 is slower), changing on to the blue metro line at the Kőbánya-Kispest terminus (the total cost is Fts 140).

By road: Hungary is presently developing a good motorway network with Budapest at its hub. Motorways include the M1 from Vienna, M7 from Lake Balaton, M5 from the south and M3 from the east of the country. The ring road around Budapest is numbered M0. The speed limit on motorways is 120km/h (75mph), on highways 100km/h (60mph), on other roads 80km/h (50mph) and in built-up areas 50km/h (30mph). Note that in Budapest, trams always have priority over other traffic. Drinking and driving don't go together in Hungary – even the smallest amount of alcohol in the blood can have you convicted.

By rail: Budapest is well served by international trains from the capitals of neighbouring countries – Vienna is approximately three hours away, Prague 7½ hours and Bratislava 2 hours and 40 minutes. Most international trains to Budapest arrive at the Keleti (Eastern) station; other Budapest stations are the Nyugati (Western) and Déli (Southern).

By bus: Long-distance buses connect Budapest with the rest of Europe. Eurolines operates a thrice-weekly year-round service from London via Vienna and Győr, increasing to five times a week in the summer peak. In Budapest, buses arrive and depart at Volánbusz coach station in Erzsébet tér.

By river: A hydrofoil service operates daily from early spring to late autumn (twice-daily from late July to early September) along the Danube River to Budapest from Vienna via Bratislava. The 282km (175-mile) journey from Vienna to Budapest takes 5½ hours; the return trip

Budapest at a Glance

upriver takes 6 hours and 20 minutes. There is also a river service that goes to Budapest from Esztergom, on the Danube Bend.

GETTING AROUND

You are bound to use Budapest's super-efficient public transport system during your stay. Tickets can be purchased at a metro station, tobacco kiosk or news stand (but not on trams or buses) and cost Fts 90; a day ticket costs Fts 700 and three-day ticket Fts 1400. Longer duration passes cost Fts 1750 for a week, Fts 2250 for two weeks or Fts 3400 for a month – for these a passport-sized photo is required. Various short-hop tickets are valid on the metro. The **Budapest Card** covers three days' unlimited travel on public transport, including the HÉV suburban railway within the city limits and the Fogaskerekű cog-wheel railway; it also allows free entry to museums and galleries, discounted city sightseeing and discounts at selected shops, restaurants and swimming baths. It costs Fts 2500.
Metro: The three underground railway lines of the Budapest Metro converge at Deák tér, on the Pest side of the river. The yellow line (M1) links Vörösmarty tér in the centre of the city with Mexikói út. The red line (M2) connects the Déli (Southern) railway station and Moszkva tér, on

the Buda side, with Örs vezér tér, in an eastern Pest suburb. The blue line (M3), newest of the three, joins Kőbánya-Kispest in an industrial southeast district and Újpest-Központ in the north of the city. Trains run at intervals of up to 12 minutes – every two minutes in the rush hour – between 04:30 and 23:10. The HÉV **suburban railway** (coloured green on maps) has four lines. Three of these run on the Pest side of the city and the fourth, going from Batthyány tér on the Buda bank of the river, serves Óbuda, Aquincum and the picturesque town of Szentendre situated on the Danube Bend.
Trams and buses: Bright yellow trams and articulated 'bendy buses' feature in Budapest's urban transport system. The trams are particularly useful for journeys along the river embankments; though they no longer have an outside platform, they still provide the most enjoyable way of seeing the city.
Trolley buses – numbered from 70 onwards, as the network started operating on Stalin's 70th birthday in 1949 – are mainly found north and east of downtown Pest. Buses, which run every 10–20 minutes from 05:00 until 23:00, run throughout the city and are especially handy when negotiating Buda's hilly districts. Night

buses operate on 17 routes and carry an 'É' suffix.
The Budavári Sikló **funicular railway** saves you the walk up Castle Hill in Buda. It operates from Lánchíd, close to the river, and costs Fts 180. The Fogaskerekű **cog-wheel railway**, built in 1874 and since electrified, climbs 3.7km (2.3 miles) from Moszkva tér into the Buda Hills.
Taxis: Tales of tourist rip-offs by dodgy cabbies persist, so use only reputable companies. These include Budataxi (tel: 233 3333), City Taxi (tel: 211 1111), Fő Taxi (tel: 222 2222), Rádió Taxi (tel: 377 7777) and Tele 5 (tel: 355 5555). Steer clear of cabs with no license plate or no meter.
Car rental: All the leading international car rental companies are represented in Budapest, along with a good spread of local firms. With its comprehensive public transport system, the Hungarian capital renders car hire largely unnecessary – unless you want to make excursions into the countryside. International car-hire companies include the following: Avis, V Szervita tér 8 (tel: 118 4240); Budget, I Krisztina körút 41–43 (tel: 356 6333); and Hertz, V Aranykéz utca 4–8 (tel: 296 0999) – they also have rental desks at the airport. Among local car-hire firms, a reliable one is Inka, located at V Bajcsy-Zsilinszky út 16 (tel: 317 2150).

Budapest at a Glance

Long before the fall of the Iron Curtain, Budapest offered its visitors a choice of hotel accommodation unrivalled by any other city in eastern Europe. International names – such as Hyatt, Inter-Continental, Ramada, Hilton and Forum – were complemented by properties of Hungary's own Danubius and Hungar Hotels chains. During the 1990s the hotel range expanded further with the addition of many three-star 'panzió' (pension) properties, popular with city-break visitors seeking less expensive but nonetheless comfortable accommodation. Note that there are fewer hotels on the Buda side of the river.

LUXURY

Atrium Hyatt, Roosevelt tér 2, 1051 Budapest, tel: 266 1234, fax: 266 9101 (Pest V). This hotel's square-block exterior conceals a spacious atrium lobby complete with a suspended replica of an early Hungarian aircraft dating from 1911. This is one of Budapest's first five-star hotels, with an outstanding riverside location.

Budapest Hilton, Hess András tér 1–3, 1014 Budapest, tel: 488 6600, fax: 488 6644 (Buda I). Situated in the heart of Buda's old Castle District, the five-star Hilton with its copper-coloured glass façade offers remarkable Danube views. The hotel also incorporates part of a Dominican church and monastery.

Corinthia Aquincum, Árpád fejedelem útja 94, 1036 Budapest, tel: 436 4100, fax: 436 4156 (Óbuda III). Modern five-star hotel facing Margaret Island, close to the site of the former Roman garrison. It offers reliable access to the city centre by suburban railway.

Danubius Gellért, Szent Gellért tér 1, 1111 Budapest, tel: 385 2200, fax: 466 6631 (Pest XI). A Budapest landmark near Szabadság híd (Liberty Bridge), the four-star Gellért has welcomed the rich and famous for more than 80 years. The hotel boasts an elegant façade and splendid thermal pool, which guests may use free.

Danubius Grand Margitsziget, Margitsziget, 1138 Budapest, tel: 329 2300, fax: 329 2429 (Margaret Island XIII). The former Ramada Grand, built more than a century ago, is situated on leafy Margaret Island, a short distance upriver from the city centre. Guests can share the comprehensive spa facilities of the adjacent Danubius Thermal Margitsziget.

Kempinski Corvinus, Erzsébet tér 7–8, 1051 Budapest, tel: 429 3777, fax: 429 4777 (Pest V). Strikingly modern and centrally located five-star hotel close to the Váci utca shopping area. Hugely expensive, it offers the very highest standards of service and cuisine.

Radisson SAS Beké, Terez korut 43, 1067 Budapest, tel: 301 1600, fax: 301 1615 (Pest VI). Opened in 1914, this four-star hotel retains an atmosphere of traditional elegance. It is handy for the new shopping and commercial development which is located at the Nyugati (Western) rail station.

MID-RANGE

Alba, Apor Péter utca 3, 1011 Budapest, tel: 375 9244 (Buda I). This modern three-star hotel is situated near the Chain Bridge at the foot of Castle Hill.

Astoria, Kossuth utca 19, 1053 Budapest, tel: 317 3411, fax: 318 6798 (Pest V). Traditional four-star hotel in late 19th-century style, situated right in the centre of Pest. It was built on the site of Budapest's former medieval walls and is well-known for its fine coffee house.

Budapest, Szilágyi E. fasor 47, 1026 Budapest, tel: 202 0044, fax: 212 2729 (Buda II). Cylinder-shaped tower in an attractive setting beneath the Buda Hills. It is situated close to the Fogaskerekű cog-wheel railway. There are good views from all the rooms of either the city or the hills.

Budapest at a Glance

Danubius Thermal Hotel Helia, Kárpát utca 62-64, 1133 Budapest,tel: 452 5800; fax: 452 5801 (Pest XIII). This large modern four-star hotel faces Margaret Island across the Danube. There are lots of spa-related facilities, including indoor pool, thermal baths and Finnish sauna. There are also rooms for handicapped guests.

Danubius Thermal Margitziget, Margitziget, 1138 Budapest, tel: 452 6200, fax: 452 6261 (Margaret Island XIII). Four-star thermal spa hotel of the Danubius Group in which huge sums were invested in 2000/01. Thermal pools and a wide range of health and fitness facilities at one of Hungary's leading spa properties.

Dunapart, Szilágyi D. tér, 1011 Budapest, tel: 355 9001, fax: 355 3770 (Buda I). This is a 32-cabin boat on the Buda side of the river, facing the Parliament building.

Erzsébet, Károlyi Mihály utca 11–15, 1053 Budapest, tel: 328 5700; fax: 328 5763 (Pest V). Three-star hotel handily placed for Váci utca shopping street. Its appealing restaurant serves Hungarian specialities; there is also a pub dispensing draught beer.

Grand Hotel Hungaria, Rákóczi út 90, 1074 Budapest, tel: 478 1100; fax: 478 1111 (Pest VII). Large 500-room four-star hotel on a main thoroughfare within easy distance of Keleti (east) station. The restaurant has live gypsy music; there is also an ice cream parlour.

Ibis Centrum, Ráday utca 6, 1094 Budapest, tel: 215 8585, fax: 215 8787 (Pest IX). The rooms in this hotel are stylishly decorated in peach and aquamarine.

K+K Opera, Révay utca 24, 1065 Budapest, tel: 269 0222, fax: 269 0230 (Pest VI). Opera buffs and art lovers will appreciate this Austrian-managed four-star hotel – it is just 50 metres from the Opera House, with works of art in every bedroom.

Nemzeti, József körút 4, 1088 Budapest, tel: 303 9310, fax: 314 0019 (Pest VIII). Centrally located Art Nouveau-style three-star on Blaha Lujza tér in Pest. Built in the 1880s, the 76-room hotel has recently undergone a major refurbishment.

Park Hotel Flamenco, Tas vezér utca, 1113 Budapest, tel: 372 2000, fax: 365 8007 (Buda XI). A modern hotel in the residential district on the Buda side, away from the city-centre bustle but convenient for the sights.

Stadion, Ifjúság útja 1-3, 1148 Budapest, tel: 251 2222; fax: 251 2062 (Pest XIV). Modern 365-room three-star hotel a bit out of town, near the Népstadion sports stadium, but close to the metro. The hotel has its own six-lane tenpin bowling alley.

Taverna, Váci utca 20, 1052 Budapest, tel: 485 3100 (Pest V). If shopping is your reason to be in Budapest, this modern four-star hotel will satisfy you – it is situated smack in the pedestrianized shopping area of Váci utca. The 222-room hotel has its own bowling alley.

BUDGET

Beatrix Panzió, Széher út 3, 1021 Budapest, tel: 275 0550, fax: 394 3730 (Buda II). This small family-run pension has 18 rooms and sits at the foot of the Buda Hills.

City Panzió Mátyás, Március 15 tér 8, 1052 Budapest, tel: 338 4711, fax: 317 9086 (Pest V). A central three-star pension near Erzsébet híd (Elizabeth Bridge), situated above the well-known Mátyás Pince restaurant, in which guests take their breakfast. Most of the rooms in the pension have views of the Danube and Buda Castle.

City Panzió Pilvax, Pilvax koz 1–3, 1052 Budapest, tel: 266 7660, fax: 317 6396 (Pest V). This modern pension is well located close to Deák tér, where the three metro lines intersect.

City Panzió Ring, Szent István körút 22, tel: 340 5450 (Pest XIII). Three-star sister to the City Panzió Mátyás, close to the Nyugati (Western) rail station. Like the Mátyás, it offers simple but good city-centre accommodation at an affordable price.

Gold Hotel Panzió, Ungvár utca 45, 1142 Budapest, tel/fax: 252 0470, 251 6282 (Pest XIV). This comfortable 22-room hotel is just a short bus ride from the Mexikói metro terminus.

Kalocsa Panzió, Kalocsai utca 85, 1141 Budapest, tel/fax: 363 2388 (Pest XIV). A comfortable hotel at an affordable price.

Orion, Döbrentei utca 13, 1013 Budapest, tel: 356 8933, fax: 375 5418 (Buda I). This family-run hotel is located on the Buda side of the Elizabeth Bridge.

Pannonia Emke, Akácfa utca 1–3, 1072 Budapest, tel: 322 9230 (Pest VII). Three-star hotel with good location just off Blaha Lujza tér in Pest.

Panzió Molnár, Fodor utca 143, 1124 Budapest, tel: 395 1872 (Buda XII). Attractively designed pension with 23 rooms. It is situated high on the Buda side of the city, a 15-minute bus ride from downtown Pest.

WHERE TO EAT

Dining out in Budapest never presents a problem. Choose Hungarian or international cuisine, or else something from the wide variety of ethnic eateries: French, Greek, Indian, Italian, Jewish, Mediterranean or Asian. Then decide on which side of

the river you intend to spend the evening – Pest offers the wider selection, but Buda rewards those prepared to travel a bit further with some really excellent venues. The restaurants of the touristy Castle District tend to be more expensive, but they are rarely disappointing. The word for restaurant is *étterem*; a *vendéglő* is often more rustic in style and cheaper, while a *bisztró* explains itself.

LUXURY

Chez Daniel, Szív utca 32, tel: 302 4039 (Pest VI). The best creative French cuisine to be found in Budapest, with the menu changing daily. Highly popular – booking is recommended.

Corvinus, Erzsébet tér 7–8, tel: 429 3777 (Pest V). A top-notch dining experience awaits at the Kempinski Corvinus Hotel – international cuisine in the elegant Corvinus restaurant and Hungarian and international offerings in the Bistro Jardin.

Gambrinus, Hotel Taverna, Váci utca 20, 1052 Budapest (Pest V). Dine well in this showpiece restaurant in the heart of Pest.

Gundel, Állatkerti körút 2, tel: 321 3550 (Pest XIV). Hungary's most famous restaurant was founded in 1894. It is extremely expensive and smart dress is *de rigueur*.

Kehli Vendéglő, Mókus utca 22, tel: 250 4241 (Buda III). More than a century old, this courtyard restaurant was reputedly a favourite of the noted Hungarian writer and gourmet Gyula Krúdy. Some way from downtown, it is located in a square of Óbuda.

Képíró, Képíró utca 3, tel: 266 0430 (Pest V). French-inspired menu; also Hungarian and international cuisine, served in stylish surroundings on two floors.

Kiskakukk, Pozsonyi út 12, tel: 239 3049 (Pest XIII). A welcoming restaurant (the name means 'little cuckoo') dispensing Hungarian and Italian flavours.

Mátyás Pince, Marcius 15 tér 8, tel: 318 1693 (Pest V). This traditional restaurant is popular with large groups. Nevertheless, it gives good service – and at acceptable prices.

Remíz, Budakeszi út 5, tel: 275 1396 (Buda II). Named after the nearby tram depot, this restaurant offers diners an interesting mix of Hungarian and international dishes on a varied menu.

Vadrózsa, Pentelei Molnár utca 15, tel: 326 5817 (Buda II). A small Baroque villa houses this highly pricey Hungarian speciality restaurant with its two dining rooms on Rózsadomb, the Hill of Roses. Dine well to a soft piano accompaniment.

Budapest at a Glance

MID-RANGE

Apostolok, Kigyó utca 4–6, tel: 267 0290 (Pest V). The neo-Gothic interior gives a church-like feel to this century-old restaurant which is located in the centre of Pest. The food is largely traditional Hungarian.

Bagolyvár, Állatkerti út 2, tel: 351 6395 (Pest XIV). The name of this restaurant literally means 'owl's castle'; this is the cosy lower-brow sister to next-door Gundel (see under Luxury) and priced accordingly, but with high standards to match.

Bombay Palace, Andrássy út 44, tel: 332 8363 (Pest VI). A member of the international chain, highly regarded for its flavours of India.

Café Pierrot, Fortuna utca 14, tel: 375 6971 (Buda I). This became Budapest's first privately owned café in 1982 and is still going strong in the city's Castle District, offering good-quality Hungarian fare to the accompaniment of piano music.

Carmel, Kazinczy utca 31, tel: 342 4585/1834 (Pest VII). This non-kosher restaurant uses traditional Jewish recipes and also serves both Hungarian and international fare. It is adjacent to the Orthodox synagogue.

Cascade, Szarvas Gábor út 8, tel: 275 2115 (Buda XII). Offers a good seafood and vegetarian selection in the Buda environs.

Dionysos, Belgrád rakpart 16, tel: 318 1222 (Pest V). Greek restaurant on the Pest riverfront decked out as a Greek village square.

Fortuna Spaten, Hess András tér 4, 1014 Budapest, tel/fax: 375 6175. Dumplings, pancakes and strudels are among the hearty Hungarian fare to be found in Buda's Castle District – wild boar, too. If you overfill, bench seats in the exit passageway can lend support.

Karpátia, Ferenciek tere 7–8, tel: 317 3596 (Pest V). Hungarian and Transylvanian fare is served here, in historic and sophisticated surroundings. The restaurant has an outside terrace; live gypsy music adds to the occasion.

Pest Buda Vendéglő, Fortuna utca 3, 1014 Budapest, tel: 212 5880 (Buda I). Ethnic Hungarian fare served in gracious surroundings in Buda's Castle District.

Replay Café, Fehér Hajó utca 12–14, tel: 266 8333. A terraced Mediterranean restaurant which has its heart firmly in Italy.

Seoul House, Fő utca 8, tel: 201 7452 (Buda I). Authentic Korean recipes give this restaurant an edge over most of the other Asian restaurants in Budapest.

Szeged, Bartók Béla út 1, tel: 209 1668 (Buda XI). This tastefully furnished eating house, with delicious fish specialities, is located to the south of Gellért Hill.

Trombitás, Retek utca 12, tel: 212 3154 (Buda II). The restaurant's genuine Hungarian ambience is an ideal setting for the nightly folk dancing display. The food here is in the best Hungarian traditions, and the location is very convenient – right on Moszkva tér.

Udvarház, Hármashatárhegy út 2, tel: 388 8780 (Buda III). Terrace dining in the Buda Hills with a dramatic overview of the city. Folklore show most evenings.

BUDGET

Fu Hao, Dózsa György út 76, tel: 342 7368 (Pest VII). A large restaurant with Chinese specialities from all parts of that country; the buffet offers 20 dishes daily.

Okay Italia, Szent István körút 20, tel: 349 2991 (Pest XIII). Lively Italian restaurant with outstanding pasta and pizza, situated near the Nyugati (Western) railway station. There is another branch close by at Nyugati tér 6, tel: 332 6960.

Tabáni Gösser, Attila út 19, tel: 375 9482 (Buda I). Hungarian and international fare on the western side of Castle Hill.

COFFEE HOUSES

They were a second home to writers and artists, poets and actors, singers and journalists – the atmospheric cafés that

Budapest at a Glance

sprang up in Budapest from the 1900s to the 1930s and earned the Hungarian capital a reputation as 'the city of coffee houses'. Nowadays elderly Hungarian ladies and visitors to the city pass time pleasantly in those coffee shops that survived the upheavals of World War II and its aftermath. Along with the coffee – a double espresso will set you up for the day – come all manner of cakes and pastries to further sweeten your day in Budapest.

Astoria, Kossuth Lajos utca 19, tel: 317 3411 (Pest V). The four-star Astoria is one of Budapest's grand late-19th/ early-20th-century hotels and the rather grand cafe with its leather-upholstered chairs well recaptures the spirit and ambience of a century ago.

Café Mozart, Erzsébet körút 36, tel: 352 0664 (Pest VI). Themed cafe where coffee is served by costumed wenches to a background of the great composer's music.

Café Pierrot, Fortuna utca 14, tel: 375 6971 (Buda I). The Pierrot was established back in the communist-ruled early 1980s as Budapest's first privately-owned cafe. It is a comfortable place in which to linger – and tuck away some local specialities if you're peckish – and there's live piano music in the evening.

Centrál Café, Károlyi Mihály utca 9, tel: 266 2110 (Pest V).

A well-known literary cafe that has been restored to its early 19th-century elegance, now a restaurant-cum-coffee shop all in one that stays open till late.

Gerbeaud, Vörösmarty tér 7, tel: 318 1311 (Pest V). This is without question Budapest's best-known coffee shop, founded by the Swiss confectioner Emile Gerbeaud in 1884, in the same building in which is it still housed today. The main coffee shop is always well populated by tourists, keen to savour *konyakos meggy* (a dark chocolate delight containing a sour cherry that has been soaked in cognac).

Lukács, Andrássy út 70, tel: 302 8747 (Pest VI). Splendidly restored late 19th-century cafe with a bright interior and some excellent gilt-work – plus piano music on some weekdays.

Muvész, Andrássy út 29, tel: 352 1337 (Pest VI). This legendary chandeliered coffee house is situated almost opposite the Opera House. It serves great pastries and is strong on traditional ambience.

New York, Erzsébet körút 9–11, tel: 322 3849 (Pest VII). Rather inelegantly propped up by wooden scaffolding, as it has been since the 1990s, the Café New York, with its ornate interior, nonetheless remains a firm favourite with Budapest's literati. Caricatures

line the walls of this Budapest landmark, which enjoyed its heyday from 1910 up to the mid-1930s.

Ruszwurm, Szentháromság utca 7, tel: 375 5284 (Buda I). An appealing coffee house in Buda's Castle District – ideal for a break from sightseeing. They've been serving coffee here since the 1820s and Princess Elisabeth ('Sissy') is said to have been among its former patrons.

ENTERTAINMENT

You should never be stuck for ideas on how to make the most of your Budapest visit. When you've had your fill of sightseeing, there is a vast choice of things to do – from opera, ballet, classical concerts and folklore shows to jazz, discos, nightclubs and casinos – there is even a puppet theatre. Pick up a copy of the monthly *Where Budapest* or *Budapest Panorama* for the latest information and listings of what's happening all over town. Try to find time for a night at the **opera**; even for non-opera buffs, a visit to the State Opera House, at Andrássy út 22 (tel: 331 2550, Pest VI), is a worthwhile experience, if only to enjoy the building's sumptuous interior; the Opera House also stages performances of the State Ballet company. Other venues staging opera are the Erkel Theatre, at Köztársaság

Budapest at a Glance

tér 30 (tel: 333 0540, Pest VIII) – it is also used by the State Opera company – and Duna Palota (Duna Palace), at Zrínyi utca 5 (tel: 317 2790, Pest V), which stages classical performances of all kinds. Other theatre venues often staging **ballet** and **contemporary dance** are the Thália Theatre, at Nagymező utca 22–24 (tel: 312 4230, Pest VI); the Merlin Theatre, at Gerlóczy utca 4 (tel: 317 9338, Pest V); and Trafó, the House of Contemporary Arts, located at Liliom utca 41 (tel: 456 2040, Pest IX).

The Liszt Music Academy, at Liszt Ferenc tér 8 (tel: 342 0179, Pest VI), is Budapest's leading **concert venue**, with nightly performances in its splendid Great Hall; concerts are also given in the Budapest Congress Centre, at Jagelló út 1–3 (tel: 209 1990, Buda XII).

For **light classics**, check out the Pest Concert Hall (Pesti Vigadó), at Vigadó tér 2 (tel: 318 9903, Pest V). The Béla Bartók Memorial House, at Csalán út 29 (tel: 376 2100, Buda II) has **chamber music** performances on Friday evenings; the Comedy Theatre, located at Szent István körút 14 (tel: 329 2340, Pest XIII) is good for **operetta** performances.

Organ recitals are given in churches, among them the Matthias Church in Buda's Castle District; St Stephen's Basilica, at Szent István tér (Pest V); and the Great Synagogue, at Dohány utca 2 (Pest VII).

Performances of **traditional Hungarian folk music**, often with full gypsy orchestra, are given in the Duna Palota; in the Bábszínház, at Andrássy út 69 (tel: 321 5200, Pest VI); and in the Buda Concert Hall (Budai Vigadó), at Corvin tér (tel: 317 2754, Buda I). The latter venue also hosts the Hungarian State Ensemble of **folk dancers** and **gypsy orchestra** from April to October each year. **Musical performances** with an international flavour take place at the International Buda stage, at Tárogató út 2–4 (tel: 391 2500, Buda II); **Jewish music** and culture is celebrated in the Great Synagogue at Dohány utca 2–8 (tel: 317 2754, Pest VII).

Rock and **jazz clubs** are dotted about Budapest. Two leading concert venues are the Benczúr Club, at Benczúr utca 27 (tel: 321 7334, Pest VI) and Petőfi Hall in Városliget, the City Park (tel: 343 4327, Pest XIV). There's live jazz, too, at the basement **Jazz Cafe**, Balassi Bálint utca 25 (tel: 269 5506, Pest V) and live Latin at the **Franklin Trocadero**, Szent István korut 15 (tel: 311 4691, Pest V).

For out and out disco, try the underground **Made Inn**, Andrássy ut 112 (tel: 311 3437, Pest VI) or the highly popular **Bahnhof**, by the side of the West railway station at Váci út 1 (tel: 0620 311181, Pest VI).

If a quieter venue appeals, **Piaf** is a small nightclub in the traditional style with a small dance floor near Oktogon metro station at Nagymező utca 25 (tel: 312 3823, Pest VI).

SHOPPING

For retail therapy, stick to the Pest side of the river. You will find many of Budapest's most expensive shops on and around pedestrianized Váci utca, Petőfi Sándor utca, Régiposta utca, Haris köz, Párizsi utca and Kigyó utca, but there are numerous other stores and specialist shops lining Pest's wide boulevards. While tourists throng Váci utca and offshoot streets, locals tend to favour the ring road from the Western station towards the Petőfi Bridge. Next to the Western station, on Váci út (not to be confused with Váci utca) is the Westend Centre, one of Budapest's last major projects of the 1990s. It has one of Europe's largest shopping centres which is open from 08:00 until midnight (until 02:00 on Friday and Saturday). Two shopping malls outside the centre of town are the Duna Plaza, at Váci út 178 (Pest XIII), near Gyöngyösi utca station on the blue Metro line (shops are open 10:00–21:00),

Budapest at a Glance

and the Pólus Center, on the northeast fringes of the city at Szentmihályi út 131 (Pest XV), which is served by bus 173 from Eastern railway station. What do you buy in Hungary? Go for porcelain (Herend and Zsolnay are big names here), antiques, folk art, costumed dolls, painted eggs, books and CDs, to name but a few.

Bookshops include Irok Boltja (the Writer's Bookshop), at Andrássy út 45 (Pest VI) and Bestsellers, at Október 6 utca 11 (Pest V). Rhythm 'n' Books, at Szerb utca 21–23 (Pest V), has a selection of second-hand English-language books; further shops selling second-hand English books are found in Múzeum körút (Pest V). For a good selection of CDs, try MCD Zeneszalon, at Vörösmarty tér 1 (Pest V); MCD Amadeus, at Szende Pál utca 1 (Pest V); Rózsavölgyi Zeneműbolt, at Szervita tér 5 (Pest V) or Fotex, close by at Szervita tér 2. Though you will find **antique shops** all over the city, collectors strapped for time should head for the Pest V district, with a larg concentration of outlets in Falk

Miksa utca, near Margaret Bridge; the southern part of Váci utca; or Kossuth Lajos utca. Try Antik Bazár, Váci utca 67 (Pest V); Antik Udvar, Szent István körút 1 (Pest V); Antik Diszkont, Falk Miksa utca 22 (Pest V); and Enterieur Antikvitás, Országház utca 2 (Buda I).

The world-famous Herend and Zsolnay porcelain factories both have retail outlets in the Pest V district of Budapest – Herend is at József nádor tér 11 and Kigyó utca 5, while the Zsolnay shops can be found at Ferenciek tere 11, Kigyó utca 4 and Kristóf tér 2. The leading porcelain brands can be found in Haas and Czjzek, Bajcsy Zsilinszky út 23 (Pest VI). Having no doubt acquainted yourself with some fine **wines** during your stay, you will want to take some home – good outlets include Weinhaus, Jókai tér 7 (Pest VI); Budapest Weingesellschaft, Batthyány utca 59 (Buda I) – with free wine-tasting on Saturday afternoons; Le Sommier IV, Régiposta utca 14 (Pest V), and House of Hungarian Wine, Szentháromság tér 6 (Buda I).

Golfers will find the Budapest Golf Park & Country Club (tel: 317 6025) 35km (22 miles) north in the Danube Bend region. The 18-hole Pannon Golf & Country Club (tel: 22/243243) is 40km (25 miles) west at Alcsútdoboz-Máriavölgy; both are open from March to October.

Tennis centres are dotted about the city – two popular venues are the Margaret Island Athletics Centre (tel: 329 3147), with four courts, and Budapest Sports Club at Szamos utca (tel: 317 4762, Pest XII), with 10 courts.

Squash courts can be found at the Budapest Marriott Hotel, Apáczai Csere utca (tel: 266 4290); the City Squash Club, at Marcibányi tér 13 (tel: 325 0082, Buda II); and the Griff Squash & Fitness Club, Bartók Béla út 152 (tel: 206 4065, Buda XI). **Tenpin bowling** venues include the Bowling Centre, Váci út 178 (Pest XIII); the Novotel, Alkotás utca 63-67 (Buda XII); Strike Bowling Club, Budafoki út 111–113 (Buda XI) and Taverna Bowling Bar (Váci utca 20, Pest V). If you want to go **horse riding**, contact the Budapest-Aranypatkó Riding School, at Aranyhegyi út 18 (tel: 387 7152, Obuda III); the Budapest Riding Club, Kerepesi út 7 (tel: 313 5210, Pest VIII); or Petneházy Riding School, Feketefej utca 2-4 (tel: 397 5048, Buda II).

BUDAPEST	J	F	M	A	M	J	J	A	S	O	N	D
AVERAGE TEMP. °F	30	35	40	53	60	68	70	71	64	53	43	35
AVERAGE TEMP. °C	-1	1	6	12	16	20	21	22	18	12	6	2
HOURS OF SUN DAILY	2	3	5	7	8	9	10	9	7	5	2	1
RAINFALL in	1.5	1.7	1.5	1.8	2.8	2.7	2.2	1.9	1.3	2.2	2.8	1.8
RAINFALL mm	37	44	38	45	72	69	56	47	33	57	70	46
DAYS OF RAINFALL	13	12	11	11	13	13	10	9	7	10	14	13

Budapest at a Glance

TOURS AND EXCURSIONS

Budatours offers a two-hour city tour with headphone commentary in 16 languages, including English; tours depart from Roosevelt tér. **Budapest Sightseeing** has a three-hour city tour in 12 languages, including 'live' in English; tours depart from the bus station in Erzsébet tér. **Cityrama** will collect you from your hotel for its three-hour city tour which departs from near the Parliament building. **Queenybus** includes a Parliament visit on its three-hour city tour departing from Szent István tér. The city tours follow a broadly similar route, covering the Castle District, the Royal Castle and the Citadel on Gellért Hill on the Buda side, and tracking through Pest, taking in the Parliament building, the Opera House and St Stephen's Basilica to Heroes' Square.
Other excursions available from the main operators include a tour of the Parliament building, a visit to Jewish Budapest, the Statue Park, Szentendre and the Danube Bend, the Baroque chateau at Gödöllő, dinner in the Buda Hills, Danube River cruises, and a day at a spa on Margaret Island.

City tours
Budapest Sightseeing, Ferenciek tere 10 (Pest V), tel: 485 2762 or 317 7767.

Budatours, Andrássy út 2 (Pest V), tel: 331 1585, 353 0558, or 312 4037.
Cityrama, Báthory utca 22 (Pest V), tel: 302 4382.
Queenybus, Törökbálinti út 28 (Buda XI), tel: 247 7159.
Jewish Budapest tours
Chosen Tours, Pagony utca 40 (Buda XII), tel: 355 2202.
Cityrama, Báthory utca 22 (Pest V), tel: 302 4382.

USEFUL CONTACTS

Tourist Information
For further information and advice on Budapest, contact **Tourinform** offices at Sütő utca 2 (Pest V), tel: 317 9800 (open 09:00–19:00; Sat–Sun 09:00–16:00); **Nyugati (Western) Railway Station**, Main Hall by platform 10 (Pest XIII), tel: 302 8580 (open 07:00–20:00); Király utca 93 (Pest VII), tel: 352 1433 (open 08:00–20:00); or Castle Hill, Tárnok utca 9–11 (Buda I), tel: 488 0453 (open 08:00–20:00). Or write to the **Budapest Tourism Office**, Pf 215, 1364 Budapest, fax: 0036 1 266 7477.

Other
AIDS helpline (in English), tel: 166 9283.
Autoclub emergency (in English), tel: 088.
Útinform (traffic information, in English), tel: 322 2238.
Thermal baths, Gellért, tel: 466 6166; Király, tel: 202 3688; Rác, tel: 356 1322;

Rudas, tel: 356 1322; Széchenyi, tel: 321 0310 or 342 8976.
Jegyiroda ticket service, tel: 317 7736 or 338 2237.
VAT refunds – Global Refund, Bég utca 3–5 (Buda II), tel: 212 4906; Intel Trade Rt, Csalogány utca 6–10 (Buda I), tel: 356 9800.
Airport – Ferihegy 2, tel: 296 9696; arrivals, tel: 296 8000; departures, tel: 296 7000; lost property, tel: 296 8108.
Taxis – Budataxi, tel: 233 3333; City Taxi, tel: 211 1111; Fő Taxi, tel: 222 2222; Rádió Taxi, tel: 377 7777; Tele 5, tel: 355 5555.
Bus information – Erzsébet tér bus station, tel: 317 2562 (international), tel: 317 2966 (domestic); Népstadion bus station, tel: 252 4498; Árpád híd bus station (for Danube Bend), tel: 329 1450.
Train information – tel: 461 5500 (international); 461 5400 (domestic).
BKV (Budapest public transport) information, tel: 342 2335.
MAHART (Hungarian Shipping Company), tel: 318 1223.
International hydrofoil services, tel: 318 1743.
Ambulance, tel: 104 (if unavailable, 311 1666).
Police, tel: 107 (if unavailable, the emergency-only numbers are 318 0800 or 311 8668).
Fire brigade, tel: 105 (if unavailable, 321 6216).

3
Danube Bend

Some 40km (25 miles) north of Budapest, the Danube is forced to abandon its easterly flow and cut south between the Börzsöny and Pilis Hills towards Budapest and southern Hungary. This section of the river, known as the **Danube Bend** (though you won't find it identified on maps as such), is one of its most scenic of the river's entire 3000km (1875-mile) length and contains an assortment of attractive towns and villages. It is a popular getaway destination among Budapest dwellers and makes an ideal extension to a city break or a long day trip from the capital.

The quaint artists' town of **Szentendre** (it means St Andrew) is just 40 minutes from the centre of Budapest by HÉV suburban train. It sits on the right bank and faces Szentendre Island – a long, thin strip of land that splits the Danube in two from Visegrád right to the outskirts of Budapest.

Upstream on the left bank is the old town of **Vác**; further along on the right bank tiny **Visegrád**, surmounted by its impressive castle. The western gateway to the Danube Bend is **Esztergom**, with its mighty basilica, and all around are the tree-clad slopes of the **Pilis** and **Börzsöny** hills – splendid country for hiking on marked trails or horse riding.

In the Pilis Hills you may catch sight of wild boar or red deer among the beech and oak woods – **Dobogókő** has been the hiking centre of the hills for more than a century. The Börzsöny Hills rise to 939m (3080ft) **Mount Csóványos** – a real mountain by Hungarian standards.

DON'T MISS

*** Esztergom: home to a spectacular basilica.
*** Szentendre: explore the old artists' colony and the Ethnographical Museum.
** Visegrád: a magnificent citadel and the ruins of the Royal Palace.
** Pilis Hills: an excellent location for hiking.
** Danube: take a MAHART river trip from Budapest to the Danube Bend towns.
* Vác: an elegant old town on the northern bank.

Opposite: *Vác Cathedral is an early example of neo-classical style.*

Danube Bend

SZENTENDRE

Szentendre never fails to please. Situated just 20km (12 miles) from the centre of Budapest, this colourful Baroque **artists' colony** turned tourist town can trap visitors for hours in its narrow streets. What may come as a surprise is Szentendre's **Serbian** connection – the town was settled by successive waves of Serbian refugees fleeing the Turks up to the late 17th century and their legacy remains in Serbian churches. Today only a handful of Serbian families remain in Szentendre.

Heading from the HÉV station, you first pass the **Serbian Orthodox Požarevačka Church** (1763) by the Bükkos stream on Kossuth utca; then, on your right, the **Marzipan Museum** on Dumtsa Jenő utca with its store of artistic sugared creations. The **Barcsay Collection** just beyond is dedicated to the work of Szentendre artist Jenő Barcsay (1900–88); the **Kmetty Museum**, where the street emerges on to Fő tér, has watercolours by Cubist painter János Kmetty (1889–1975).

Across the square, resplendent with its marble-based Plague Cross (1763), the **Margit Kovács Museum** down Görög utca honours one of Hungary's greatest sculptors (1902–77). On the corner of Görög utca is the **Orthodox Blagoveštenska Church** (1754), the work of Baroque architect András Mayerhoffer with icons relating to Serbian history. Next to the church at Fő tér 6, the **Ferenczy Museum** in a former Serbian school details the work of Károly Ferenczy (1862–1917), who originated the 'plein air' style of Hungarian painting.

North of the square at Bogdányi utca 12, close to the Wine Museum, is the **Imre Ámos–Margit Anna Museum**, with its Symbolist paintings of 1930s and 1940s; from here head left up Castle Hill, once topped by a medieval fortress, to the **Parish Church of St John** in Templom tér, where a craft market is held in summer. At

---

OPEN-AIR MUSEUM

The enormous open-air **Ethnographical Museum** (*skanzen*) – 3km (2 miles) northwest of Szentendre on the slopes of Pismán Hill – is the biggest of its kind in Hungary. It covers 46ha (113 acres) and is being developed with some 340 buildings grouped in 10 regions to reflect all styles of traditional Hungarian architecture – four regions had been completed at the time of writing: Upper Tisza in Northeast Hungary, Kisalföld and Orség in Western Transdanubia, and the Great Plain.

Templom tér 1, the **Czóbel Museum** has paintings by impressionist Béla Czóbel (1883–1976).

Just to the north, the dark red church at Alkotmány utca is the Baroque-Rococo **Belgrade Cathedral**, built in the 1760s and the headquarters of the Serbian Orthodox church in Hungary. The adjacent **Serbian Ecclesiastical Collection** contains items collected from redundant Serbian churches in the country.

VISEGRÁD

Though home to only 2000 people, Visegrád (the name means 'high castle') is enormously significant in Hungarian history. It was a royal fortress from the 13th century and today contains three key elements – the Citadel high on a 300m (1000ft) crag above the Danube, Solomon's Tower (*see* panel, this page) and the excavations of the Royal Palace.

The magnificent **Citadel**, best viewed from the opposite bank, was started by Béla IV in 1242 in anticipation of further Mongol incursions; he also built a lower castle, which evolved into the **Royal Palace** under King Charles Robert of Anjou some 80 years later. Expansion of the Gothic palace was ongoing through the years, with King Matthias Corvinus and Queen Beatrice ordering its rebuilding in Renaissance style in the late 15th century.

Excavation and partial reconstruction of the palace, once said to be the finest in Europe, are ongoing. The **Lion Fountain** is a replica, the **Court of Honour** and foundations, including those of the chapel, reconstructions. High walls were built to join the upper citadel and palace over a period of two centuries; a model within the citadel shows how they were linked.

Below: *Those with a sweet tooth will satisfy their craving in the Marzipan Museum shop.*

CARDINAL MINDSZENTY

The tomb of Hungary's heroic primate, Cardinal József Mindszenty (1892–1975), is in the crypt beneath Esztergom's mighty basilica. Opposing secularized education under the communists, Mindszenty was tortured and sentenced to life imprisonment for treason, but released in the 1956 Uprising; he took refuge in the US Embassy in Budapest for 15 years and died in Austria in 1975. Although he had vowed not to return to Hungary until after the last Russian soldier had left, his body was returned in 1991 before the Pope's visit – some weeks before the Russians' final exit.

The citadel stored Hungary's crown jewels until they were stolen in the mid-15th century; today it houses small displays and exhibits. Climb the tower, investigate the interior and walk the ramparts for spectacular views of the Danube and the Börzsöny Hills. You can hike up to the citadel along a trail marked 'Fellegvár', which you can join behind the church or at **Solomon's Tower**.

ESZTERGOM

You perceive the green dome of Esztergom's mighty neo-Classical **Basilica** towering above the city long before you reach it. The seat of Catholicism in Hungary, it occupies the site where Esztergom-born King Stephen I was crowned on Christmas Day 1000. Its dimensions are vast – 118m (387ft) by 40m (131ft), surmounted by a dome which is 72m (236ft) high.

The basilica's originators in 1822 were **Pál Kühneland** and **János Packh**; **József Hild**, designer of Eger's cathedral, was involved in its completion by 1869. The

cathedral had been consecrated 13 years before, with a Mass composed by Liszt. Don't miss the striking copy of Titian's *Assumption* over the main alter. The **Bakócz Chapel** in red and white marble is to the left of the entrance and the basilica's treasury to the right. Climb to the bell tower and to the cupola for superb views of the city.

Immediately south of the basilica – on the site of the Roman fortress of Solva Mansio – is the reconstructed former **Royal Palace**, originally built by Béla III and used by Hungarian monarchs for 300 years until capital status switched to Buda. It was subsequently the archbishop's seat until its destruction by the Turks and now houses the **Castle Museum** in a number of restored rooms.

Below the castle ramparts, the compact **Víziváros** (Watertown) district has some points of interest – highlights include the Italianate **Parish Church** from 1738, the Renaissance former **Bishop's Palace** housing the **Christian Museum** (*see* panel, this page) and the **Bálint Balassi Museum**, named after the poet killed in the bid to wrest Esztergom Castle from Turkish hands in 1594.

VÁC

Vác is the largest settlement on the left bank of the Danube, its elegant three-cornered square, Március 15 tér, a short walk from the long, leafy Danube promenade facing Szentendre Island. Around the flower-decked square, the colourful and elegant buildings include the Baroque **Dominican Church** on the south side; the former **Bishop's Palace** – home to an institute for the deaf and dumb for the past 200 years – on the east side and Baroque **Town Hall** (1764) along its western edge.

The seals on the Town Hall are those of Hungary and Bishop Kristóf Migazzi, who masterminded the late 18th-century rebuilding of Vác and subsequently became Archbishop of Vienna. The **Triumphal Arch**, north on Dózsa György út, was the inspiration of Migazzi for the

Above: *The Esztergom Basilica is the seat of Catholicism in Hungary.*
Opposite: *Solomon's Tower in Visegrád.*

CHRISTIAN MUSEUM

The former Bishop's Palace in Esztergom's Víziváros (Watertown) district contains the outstanding Christian Museum, housing Hungary's most valuable array of medieval art treasures. They include a 15th-century *Calvary* altar panel by **Tamás Kolozsvári** and exquisite *Holy Sepulchre* of **Garam-szentbenedek**, a gilded carving on wheels from 1480 depicting Christ's tomb guarded by the Apostles and Roman soldiers – it is used in Easter Week parades. There are also works of Dutch, German and Italian masters.

Above: *The Dominican Church in the centre of Vác is a fine example of ornate Baroque.*

visit of Maria Theresa in 1764; Hungary's only such monument, it is now dwarfed by the massive bulk of the town's prison. Founded as an academy by Maria Theresa it later became a barracks and still serves as a penal institution today.

Vác's other key building is its **Cathedral** on Konstantin tér – completed in the 1770s to the design of French architect Isidore Canevale, it was one of Hungary's first neo-Classical buildings and is fronted by huge Corinthian columns. The excellent altar and dome frescoes are by Franz Anton Maulbertsch.

Some 20km (12 miles) upriver from Vác is peaceful **Nagymaros**, where often the only sound to be heard is domestic dogs in conversation with canine compatriots across the river in Visegrád. The view of Visegrád's citadel from here is truly spectacular; prior to 1989, when work was abandoned in the face of sustained protest, Nagymaros was to have been the site of a major hydro-electric dam project.

In neighbouring **Zebegény**, the **Catholic Church** designed by Károly Kos and completed in 1914 is the only Hungarian church in the National Romantic style. An oddity here is the tiny **Museum of Navigation and Seafaring People**, a few minutes' walk from the village centre at Szonyi utca 9, housing the personal collection of Captain Vince Farkas.

TAKE TO THE HILLS

The limestone hills of the Pilis range rise to 756m (2480ft) in the south of the Danube Bend region and contain the protected 32,000ha (79,000-acre) Pilis Park Forest, a former medieval hunting ground. Marked trails offer easy and difficult hikes and the paths offer grand views of the river; the hills of oak and beech are also excellent for bird-watching. Dobogókő makes a good hiking base and can be reached by bus from Pomáz station on the HÉV rail line between Budapest and Szentendre.

Danube Bend at a Glance

The towns and villages of the Danube Bend really come alive in **summer**, when visitors are many. The changing colours of the Börzsöny and Pilis hills make **autumn** good for hiking north and south of the Danube.

The HÉV **suburban train** runs from Batthyány tér station in Budapest to Szentendre at roughly 20-minute intervals; **trains** for Esztergom and Vác depart from Budapest-Nyugati station. **Buses** run from Árpád Bridge bus station in Budapest, on the blue metro line, to Szentendre, Vác, Visegrád and Esztergom – there are services to Esztergom from many points in Transdanubia. MAHART runs **river boats** and **hydrofoils** the length of the Danube Bend, from Budapest to Esztergom.

There are good **road** and **rail** connections along both banks of the Danube. **Ferries** cross the river at regular intervals, usually hourly; there is also a ferry to Esztergom from Štúrovo in Slovakia.

Esztergom
MID-RANGE
Esztergom Hotel, Prímás sziget, Nagy-Duna sétány, tel/fax: 33 412 555. Modern three-star hotel where Little Danube meets its big sister; reputation for friendly service.

Zebegény
Mid-range
Kenderes, Dózsa György út 26, 2627 Zebegény, tel: 06 27 373 444; fax: 06 27 373 469. Delightful modern 24-room three-star hotel on the Danube's north bank.

Visegrád
MID-RANGE
Silvanus, Pf. 24, 2025 Visegrád, tel: 26 398 311. Three-star hotel near hilltop citadel. Great views over the Danube; tennis and squash. **Vár**, Fő utca 9, 2025 Visegrád, tel: 06 26 397 522; fax: 06 26 397 572. Stylish riverside three-star with its own sauna beneath Solomon's Tower.

Esztergom
MID-RANGE
Prímás Pince, Szent István tér 4, 2500 Esztergom, tel: 33 400 063. Beneath the road to the basilica, it boasts a high vaulted ceiling. The moderately priced food is good, too.

Szentendre
MID-RANGE
Százéves Sólyom, Dumtsa Jenő utca 7, 2000 Szentendre, tel: 26 311 484. Try the apple cream soup, catfish fillet and vegetable ragout. Delicious.

Visegrád
MID-RANGE
Gulyás Csárda, Nagy Lajos Király utca 4, 2025 Visegrád, tel: 06 26 398 329. Goulash

and many other Magyar dishes are served in this appealing village-centre restaurant. **Renaissance**, Fő utca 11, 2025 Visegrád, tel: 26 398 081. This restaurant exudes medieval ambience with its costumed waiters and wenches, its clay plates and goblets. Don a cardboard crown and feast like a king.

Vác
MID-RANGE
MoMo, Timár utca 9, 2600 Vác, tel: 27 306 777. Trout, monkfish, tuna, salmon, shark and catfish down by the river in Vác; a favourite with business locals.

MAHART **river boats** are timetabled to give Budapest folk a day on the Danube Bend, rather than vice versa. But river boat excursions within the Danube Bend region between Esztergom and Szentendre allow several hours ashore.

For further information on Danube Bend resorts, contact **Tourinform** offices at Szentendre (Dumtsa Jenő utca 22, 2000 Szentendre, tel: 26 317 965) and Vác (Dr Csányi körút 45, 2600 Vác, tel: 27 316 160). In Esztergom, information offices include **Gran Tours**, at Széchenyi tér 25 (tel: 33 313 756).

4
Lake Balaton

Lake Balaton is known as the 'Hungarian sea'. It is Europe's largest freshwater lake outside Scandinavia, a stand-in seashore and pleasure ground for millions of summer visitors who throng the necklace of bustling **resorts** large and small around its perimeter.

Nearly 80km (50 miles) long and ranging in width from 1.5km (1 mile), where the **Tihany Peninsula** almost splices it, to 14km (9 miles) at its widest point, Lake Balaton is the playground of both Hungary and neighbouring countries of central Europe. In communist times, it served as 'neutral territory' on which East and West Germans could mingle – the larger part of today's foreign visitors are eastern Germans revisiting favourite haunts along the lake.

Lake Balaton's northern and southern shores offer contrasting scenery. **North of Balaton** is hilly, the south-facing slopes covered with vineyards that produce most of the region's quality wines; reed beds and stretches of green shoreline separate the resorts. The **southern slopes** are gentler; here the water is much shallower, the resorts run into one another and you are unaware just where one place ends and another begins.

Railway lines link the resorts of both the northern and southern shores with Budapest – useful if you want to travel back and forth across the lake on the MAHART boats and don't have to return to your starting point. In high summer, a service operates the length of the lake between Balatonkenese and Keszthely – the trip takes five hours and stops are made on both sides of the lake.

DON'T MISS

*** Tihany: visit the lovely twin-spired Abbey Church.
** Veszprém: one of the country's oldest cities, just north of Lake Balaton.
** Hévíz: have a soak in the thermal lake at the spa.
** Keszthely: visit the neo-Baroque Festetics Palace.
* Balatonfüred: take a leisurely stroll along the shady Tagore promenade.
* Badacsony: a wine region renowned for its vineyards.
* Siófok: Balaton's largest resort is bright and breezy.

Opposite: *Lake Balaton is the 'seaside' for landlocked Hungarians.*

COME TO THE BALL

The big social occasion of the year on Lake Balaton is the **Anna Ball** at Balatonfüred, held by tradition on a Saturday in mid to late July. The first Anna Ball was staged in the Horváth House at Gyógy tér 3 – the building was formerly a hotel – on 26 July 1825. It has since moved around a number of venues, latterly to the Sanatorium and the Annabella Hotel. A Queen of the Ball is elected each year.

FAVOURITE FISH

The *fogas*, or **pike-perch**, is indigenous to Balaton and is among the tastiest of the 42 species of fish to be found in the lake. You will find *fogas* (strangely, the name means 'rack' in Hungarian) on pretty well every restaurant menu in the region – oven-roasted, grilled and with various sauces. Other Balaton fish include *harcsa* (catfish) and *ponty* (carp).

THE NORTHERN SHORE
Tihany

The heavily wooded Tihany Peninsula, jutting far out into the lake, fully merits its popularity as one of Hungary's tourism honey-pots – for visitor numbers outside Budapest it rivals Szentendre on the Danube Bend (*see page 76*).

The crowning glory of Tihany is the Baroque twin-spired **Abbey Church**, built in 1754 on the site of a Benedictine abbey founded in 1055 – the original crypt containing the tomb of King Andrew I can be visited beneath the church. Within, the beautifully carved altars, screens, organ and pulpit are the work of Sebastian Stuhlhof; his fiancée, who died young, is said to be represented by the angel to the right of St Mary's altar (on your left as you face the magnificent main altar).

The church was largely restored in 1889, when the inspired ceiling frescoes were added. The **Benedictine Abbey Museum** contains a history of the church and a room dedicated to Charles IV, the last Hungarian king.

From the church, the **Pisky sétány** promenade leads past the **Open-air Museum**, featuring restored 18th-century houses, and the **Dolls Museum** to **Echo Hill**. By throwing your voice at the church wall you can hear the echo – if you're lucky, a party of shrill-pitched schoolchildren may already be testing their vocal chords.

You can either hike further into the peninsula along one of several colour-coded trails – or return to the **Pottery House** at Batthyány utca 26 to admire the

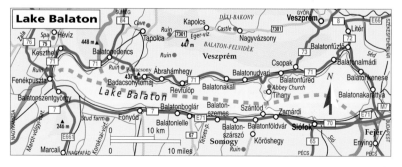

remarkable selection of jugs, plates and jars for sale, many of them heavily glazed in rich blue and green. You'll find the Pottery House behind the Open-air Museum.

Much of the Tihany Peninsula is a **nature reserve**, with the Inner Lake filling its volcanic crater visible below the village. Cut into the basalt cliffs are cells of the Orthodox monks who settled on the peninsula in the 11th century; there are exceptional views from the **Aranyház geyser cone** of both the Inner Lake and the Outer Lake, now a nesting ground for many bird species.

Buy your presents and Hungarian holiday souvenirs in Tihany village – embroidery, pottery, lace, hand-painted eggs, strings of paprika and garlic and a huge wine selection for which Tihany and the Balaton area at large are renowned. Eat well, too, in one of the restaurants tucked away in tiny hidden courtyards. A small 'road train' offers trips round the peninsula.

Above: *Bust of the 19th-century Romantic novelist Mór Jokai in his former villa in the resort of Balatonfüred.*

Balatonfüred

North-east of Tihany is Balatonfüred, regarded as the 'capital' of Lake Balaton. It's the oldest and largest resort on the north shore of the lake, where the well-to-do of the 19th century built their villas and where today Hungarians and foreign visitors – mostly Germans – mingle along the shady **Tagore Promenade**. The walkway was named

Above: *Sunbathing by the lake in the resort of Balatonudvari.*

after the Nobel Prize winner Rabrindranath Tagore, who recovered from illness in the fashionable spa resort. Near the promenade, trees that were planted by Tagore and other notables as thanks for their treatment are marked by plaques.

A **museum** dedicated to Hungary's great Romantic novelist **Mór Jokai** (1825–1904), in his former Eclectic-style villa just up from the pier, contains some of his original furniture and belongings. At the end of Blaha Lujza utca, in the middle of Gyógy tér (Health Square), is the **Kossuth Well**, where you can have your fill of the curative sulphur-tasting spa water that launched Balatonfüred 300 years ago. The waters aid those with heart problems – hence the existence of the large cardiac **hospital** along the square's eastern side; the striking pink and gold building on the north side is the **Sanatorium**.

Close to Balatonfüred heading towards the north are peaceful **Csopak**, noted for its wine-tasting cellars, and **Balatonalmádi**, a spa town since 1877, with the northern shore's longest beach and buildings of red Permian sandstone. These include the **Chapel of the Holy Right**, next to Szent Imre Church; the building was originally sited within the Royal Palace in Budapest and contained the mummified right hand of St Stephen – Hungary's holy relic is now in St Stephen's Basilica in Budapest (*see* page 53).

West of Tihany

On the other side of the Tihany Peninsula, the northern shore has spawned a ribbon of small resorts, each with its own grassy lakeside recreation area – or strand – whose facilities you pay a token admission fee (usually around Fts 120–180) to enjoy; among these resorts are **Balatonudvari**, **Révfülöp** and **Ábrahámhegy**.

ROCKY START

From the Róza Szegedy House (a museum devoted to the actress wife of the poet Sándor Kisfaludy) above Badacsony, a path leads up to **Rózsakő** (Rose Rock). Tradition holds that if a man and a woman sit on the rock with their backs to Lake Balaton, sharing thoughts of each other, they will be married within a year. The **Kisfaludy Tower** sits on the highest point locally, at 437m (1433ft).

Further to the west, **Badacsony** is another crowd-puller – but don't be put off by the fast-food and trashy souvenir stands by the rail station. This is a renowned **wine region**, the volcanic soil producing a rich grape harvest – Badacsony's own Kéknyelű, Zöldszilváni and Szürkebarát among them. The local **museum**, at Badacsonytomaj, is dedicated to **József Egry** (1883–1951), a noted Balaton artist.

Keszthely and Hévíz

At the western end of the lake, Keszthely is not to be missed – if only for the grand neo-Baroque **Festetics Palace** in a splendid park. Count György Festetics (1755–1819) created the **Helikon Library**, with its 52,000 volumes, here and in 1797 founded Europe's first agricultural school, the **Georgikon**, with more than 100 rooms and halls. Parts of it date from 1745, though its present appearance is mostly from the 1880s.

On pedestrianized Kossuth utca, No. 22 was the birthplace of **Karl Goldmark**, composer of the opera *The Queen of Sheba*. Off Kossuth utca, the three-sided Fő tér contains the **Trinity Column**, dating from 1770, and the Baroque **Town Hall**.

Just 6km (4 miles) from Keszthely is **Hévíz**, Hungary's best-known spa. It sits by Europe's largest thermal lake where, in mineral-rich water at a constant 30°C (86°F), bathers float gently about within their rubber rings, and giant water-lilies bloom from May to November. The turreted pavilion and wooden catwalks add more than a touch of fantasy here.

> **SHORE TO SHORE**
>
> The MAHART shipping company operates an extensive network of services linking resorts along both banks and crossing the lake at several points. Boats operate from **Balatonkenese** at the lake's eastern end to **Keszthely** in the west, but the schedule does not permit an end-to-end trip in a single day. The resorts of Balatonfüred, Tihany and Badacsony on the north shore and Balatonboglár on the south bank have most departures – from 10 to 14 a day in summer.

Below: *Hévíz spa is situated by Europe's largest thermal lake.*

The flat-topped, coffin-shaped hill above Badacsony, best viewed from Lake Balaton's southern shore, is in fact an extinct volcano rising to nearly 457m (1500ft). On its south-eastern slopes is a semicircle of basalt 'organ pipes', which formed when the molten magma cooled. From near Badacsony's post office, four-wheel-drive jeeps will take you into the hills to start your hike.

THE SOUTHERN SHORE

Siófok

After the relaxed and spacious resorts of the north shore, Siófok – Balaton's **largest resort** by a long way – assails the senses with its wall-to-wall slot arcades, fast-food restaurants and cheap souvenir stands along Petőfi sétány to the east of the canal. But a glance across this particular street will reveal an altogether more illustrious past, with enormous villas, most well past their prime, tucked away behind the trees.

Though rather too brash for some, Siófok – towards the lake's eastern part at the end of motorway M7 from Budapest – is a pleasant enough spot in which to spend an afternoon. Cross the railway on Mártírok utca by the canal and another shopping spree awaits on Kálmán Imre sétány, running parallel to the tracks.

Here, at No 5, is the **Imre Kálmán Museum**, dedicated to the noted composer of operettas (1882–1953), who was born in Siófok in a house on the site – his works include *Countess Mariza* and *Queen of the Csárdás*. A short way down Hock köz brings you to Siófok's impressive wooden **water tower** on Szabadsag tér, built in 1912.

The **canal**, started by the Romans in AD292 and utilized by the Turks 1400 years later, uses the River Sió, which drains the lake into the Danube. The flow of water is controlled by lock gates.

West from Siófok

One watering place, complete with its own lakeside strand, runs into another west of Siófok. There's a broad similarity about the sequence of small resorts, most prefixed by 'Balaton-', that line the southern shoreline across the rail tracks from Route 71 which circuits the lake. Next in line comes **Zamárdi**, with the **Zamárdi Regional Museum** of folk architecture at Fő utca 83, and then **Szántódi-rév**, the car ferry crossing point for Tihany on the north shore. Here is the **Szántódpuszta** (*see* panel, opposite page), an assembly of early farm buildings.

The highlight (literally) of **Balatonföldvár** is its 20m (66ft) lookout tower dating from 1872. The resort was home to the Széchenyi family, who were responsible for the Chain Bridge in Budapest. Just 3km (2 miles) inland, the 15th-century Gothic church at **Köröshegy** stages summer concerts.

In **Balatonszárszó**, the **Attila József Memorial Museum** at József Attila utca 7 is dedicated to the noted Hungarian poet (1905–37). Next in line heading west is **Balatonszemes**, where the **Postal Museum** in an old coaching inn – complete with old horse-drawn coaches – tells the tale of Hungary's postal service.

The twin resorts of **Balatonlelle** and **Balatonboglár** are the focus of the southern shore's **wine industry**. **Fonyód**, directly across the lake from Badacsony's 'table mountain', is the largest and oldest town in the area, which shows evidence of having been settled 4000 years ago. It has some interesting villas, good beaches and an attractive harbour.

Above: *Modern sculpture tests the imagination in Balatonszárszó.*
Opposite: *Siófok's fine wooden water tower.*

At the lake's western end, a marshy region known as **Kis-Balaton** (Small Balaton) supports at least 100 bird species, of which cormorants, herons and bee-eaters are among the most common. There are two good bird hides for enthusiasts, located at **Kányavár Island** and **Pap Island**.

Bakony Hills

The Bakony Hills, to the north of Lake Balaton, contain some real finds and merit at least a day of your time, preferably more. Don't overlook **Veszprém** – one of the country's oldest cities, it staged the coronation of Hungarian queens in medieval times and became known as the 'town of queens'.

In Veszprém's historic quarter, through the **Heroes' Gate** with its **Castle Museum**, are five churches: the

---

BACK ON THE FARM

You can get a good impression of Hungarian rural activity in times past at the **Szántódpuszta**, 13km (8 miles) southwest of Siófok. Here some 30 farm buildings from the 18th and 19th centuries are preserved – sheds, barns, stables, blacksmith's shop, *csárda* (inns) and St Christopher's Chapel, dating from 1735. Horse shows are staged in summer at the *puszta's* stud farm; there is also an aquarium.

Above: *The imposing 15th-century keep of Nagyvázsony Castle.*

Cathedral of St Michael, dating in part from the early 11th century; the yellow Franciscan **St Stephen's Church**; the foundations of **St George's Chapel** (1230) beneath a protecting canopy; the **Piarist Church** (1836), and **Gizella Chapel**, named after the wife of King Stephen.

Statues of the royal couple – installed in 1938 on the 900th anniversary of King Stephen's death – are at the far end of Vár utca, from where there are fine views of the town, Valley Bridge over the Séd, and the Bakony Hills. Chimes ring over the city every hour from the **Fire Tower** – climb it for a fine perspective of the city.

Worth visiting for their castles are **Nagyvázsony** and **Sümeg**. From the 15th-century **Castle of Pál Kiniszi** (he was a favoured general of King Matthias) at Nagy-vázsony, the impressive 29m (95ft) keep survives amid ruined walls.

Sümeg Castle, atop a conical limestone hill, is men-tioned in Hungarian records of 1318; it is one of the best-preserved castles in the country.

Between Nagyvázsony and Sümeg, **Tapolca** is noted for its **Mill Lake**, complete with a water wheel, just off the town centre. The former mill is now the Gabriella Hotel.

Lake Balaton at a Glance

BEST TIMES TO VISIT

Resorts around Lake Balaton are crowded in summer, when the weather is at its sunny best. It is less crowded in June and September, but can be cooler.

GETTING THERE

The northern and southern shores of Lake Balaton have rail links to Budapest. Buses for Lake Balaton depart from the bus station on Erzsébet tér.

GETTING AROUND

MAHART boats link resorts on opposite sides of the lake; car ferries ply between Tihanyi-rév and Szántódrév, and between Badacsony and Fonyód from March to October. Rail and bus are reliable alternatives.

WHERE TO STAY

Northern Shore
MID-RANGE
Annabella, Deák Ferenc utca 25, 8231 Balatonfüred, tel: 87 342 222; fax: 87 343 084, 87 483 029. One of Balaton's largest, with 388 rooms and pool deck. Great for families.
Danubius Hotel Helikon, Balaton-part 5, 8360 Keszthely, tel: 83 311 330; fax: 83 315 403. A 232-room resort hotel right on the lake.
Panoráma, Lepke sor 9–10, 8237 Tihany, tel/fax: 87 448 494. Welcoming three-star on Tihany peninsula. Has its own private beach, water sports.
Park, Petőfi Sándor utca 26, 8380 Hévíz, tel: 83 341 190/2; fax: 83 341 193.

Charming 26-room three-star near thermal lake. Built in 1927, it has a modern extension.
Petrol, Orkény sétány 1, 8229 Csopak, tel/fax: 87 446 410. Peaceful lakeside setting, with indoor pool and tennis.

Bakony Hills
MID-RANGE
Gabriella, Batsányi tér 7, Tapolca, tel: 87 511 070, 87 412 642. Inexpensive; in converted 13th-century mill-house.

Southern Shore
MID-RANGE
Best Western Magistern, Beszédes József sétány 72, 8600 Siófok, tel/fax: 84 314 400. Modern large three-star on the edge of Siófok.
Krudy Panzió, Batthyány Lajos utca 1, 8600 Siófok, tel/fax: 84 310 416; 74 458 270. Pink and green villa with a shady garden restaurant.
Tópart, Zrínyi utca 1, 8171 Balatonvilágos, tel: 88 380 744; fax: 88 380 010. Apartment hotel at water's edge.

WHERE TO EAT

Northern Shore
MID-RANGE
Muskátli, Kossuth Lajos utca 43, Tihany, tel: 06 30 9390 561, 06 30 2268 926. Tiny courtyard restaurant. Wide menu, Balaton fish specialities.
Sramli, Pethö utca 4, Keszthely, no phone at time of writing. Courtyard restaurant with Hungarian music, great-value authentic Hungarian cuisine.

Bakony Hills
MID-RANGE
Óváros, Szabadszág tér 14, Veszprém, tel: 88 326 790. Courtyard restaurant with high reputation just outside old city.
Vazsonyko, Sörház utca 2, Nagyvázsony, tel: 88 264 344. Try *lecsó galuskával*, a ragout with egg noodles. Delicious!

Southern Shore
MID-RANGE
Étel-és Sörbár, Kálmán Imre sétány 6, Siófok, tel: 84 312 250. Inexpensive wide menu, on Siófok's shopping street.

TOURS AND EXCURSIONS

Summer cruises on Balaton from the major resorts include evening disco cruises from Balatonfüred and Siófok. MAHART **ferries** link many of the resorts – timetables are posted near boarding points.

USEFUL CONTACTS

For further information on Lake Balaton resorts, contact the respective **Tourinform** offices. These include Balatonfüred (Petőfi Sándor utca 8, 8230 Balatonfüred, tel: 87 342 237); Keszthely (Kossuth utca 28, 8360 Keszthely, tel: 83 314 144); Siófok (Viztorony, Pf. 75, 8600 Siófok, tel: 84 315 355); and Tihany (Kossuth Lajos utca 20, 8237 Tihany, tel: 87 448 804). For **Lake Balaton cruises**, contact MAHART, Krudy setany 2, 8600 Siófok, tel: 84 312 907.

5
Transdanubia

Transdanubia – 'across the Danube' – is a region of great scenic and cultural variety that covers Hungary west of the great river, comprising around two-fifths of the country's area, and contains much to delight the visitor. On your Transdanubian travels between some of Hungary's historically most important towns, you cross rolling hills, dip into valleys and cross the flat southern plains known locally as *puszta*.

This was **Pannonia** in Roman times. The empire reached to the banks of the Danube, and in its frontier province the **Romans** established key towns – among them were Arrabona (present-day Győr), Savaria (Szombathely), Scarbantia (Sopron) and Sophianae (Pécs). The castles and fortifications dotted throughout Transdanubia are strong indications of a turbulent past in which the region has been settled and resettled by successive incomers.

Unlike much of Hungary, a sizeable chunk of northern Transdanubia stayed under **Habsburg** domination during the century and a half of Turkish occupation and was spared the destruction that befell many Hungarian towns and cities. Thus smaller towns closer to Vienna, stronghold of the Habsburgs – such as Sopron and Kőszeg – have maintained their original charm.

Splitting Transdanubia into northern and southern parts is the 600km² (232 sq mile) expanse of **Lake Balaton** (*see* Chapter 4, page 82). Between Balaton and Budapest is little **Lake Velence**, which offers an alternative area of relaxation to the larger lake.

Don't Miss

*** Sopron:** take a walk around the inner town.
** Győr:** known especially for the Reliquary Bust of St László in the cathedral.
** Esterházy Palace:** grand Baroque mansion at Fertőd.
** Kőszeg:** see the coloured buildings of Jurisics tér.
** Pannonhalma:** the oft-restored Benedictine abbey.
** Pécs:** a centre with many museums and galleries.
* Nagycenk:** the site of Count István Széchenyi's neo-Classical mansion.

Opposite: *Church of St Imre in the attractive small town of Kőszeg.*

GYŐR

Chief among the cities of northern Transdanubia, Győr has the image of an industrial place as the producer of trucks and rolling stock, yet in its historical heart there is plenty to explore. Its strategic position at the confluence of the Mosoni-Duna, Rába and Rábca rivers was recognized by the Romans, who called it Arrabona; its present name stems from *gyűrű*, the Avar word for a circular fort.

Most sights of interest to the visitor are in the compact **Belváros** (inner town), behind the remodelled **Bishop's Castle** on Káptalandomb (Chapter Hill), with its 13th-century keep and 15th-century **Dóczy Chapel**. The **Cathedral**, on the site of an 11th-century Romanesque church, shows quite a broad mixture of styles – Gothic, neo-Classical and Romanesque, with a largely Baroque interior. The cathedral's 15th-century **Héderváry Chapel** contains the **Reliquary Bust of St László**, an example of the very best output of medieval goldsmiths.

The **Diocesan Treasury** and **Library** at Káptalandomb 26 boasts an impressive ecclesiastical collection. On

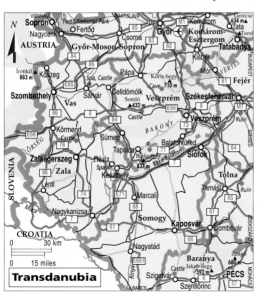

Jedlik Ányos utca, the **Margit Kovács Exhibition** contains work of this renowned Hungarian ceramicist and sculptor who was born in Győr. Follow Jedlik Ányos utca south to **Széchenyi tér**, Győr's medieval main square where historic buildings surround the **Column of the Virgin Mary**, erected in 1686 to celebrate the capture of Buda from the Turks. They include Vastuskós (Iron Stump) House at No. 4, where journeymen would hammer in a nail to mark their visit. Within its walls, the **Imre Patkó Collection** is an excellent assembly of African and Oceanic art. At No. 5, the **János Xanthus Museum** in the Baroque Abbot's House has a wide brief – local history, medical history, stamps and furniture are included. Across the square, the Benedictine **Church of St Ignatius** (1641) has an interior which was modelled on Rome's Il Gesu Church; the **Pharmacy Museum** is housed in the priory next door and is pure 17th-century Baroque.

West down Kazinczy utca you reach the **Carmelite Church** (1725) on Bécsi kapu tér, with the exquisite 18th-century *Mary of the Foam* statue in an adjacent chapel; it is said to have miraculously prevented the Rába River from flooding in the 18th century. Joined to the church is the 250-year-old convent, which now accommodates the Klastrom Hotel around its splendid inner courtyard.

Above: *A fine Carmelite Church dominates Bécsi kapu tér, Győr.*

Pannonhalma

Benedictine Pannonhalma Abbey, rebuilt and restored down the centuries in widely ranging styles, lies about 20km (12 miles) to the south of Győr on 282m (925ft) St Marton Hill. In 1996, **Pope John Paul II** celebrated the millennium of the UNESCO-listed abbey, which played a prominent role in the Christianization of Hungary. The monastery contains Hungary's only complete **medieval cloister** as well as a 360,000-volume **library**; within its archives is the foundation deed of **Tihany Abbey**, which dates from 1055 and contains the earliest examples of written Hungarian.

SZÉKESFEHÉRVÁR

This is Hungary's oldest and a historically important town, where the Magyars' leader **Árpád** first set up camp when he crossed the Danube in AD972. His great-great-grandson **Stephen I** chose Székesfehérvár (named after the white castle, or *fehérvár* of his father, Prince Géza) to be his seat, and over a period of almost 500 years, 37 Hungarian kings and 39 queens were crowned here in its **basilica**.

The basilica's excavated foundations – St Stephen, founder of the Hungarian state, was buried here in 1038 – can be seen in the **Romkert** (Garden of Ruins). Stones from the ruined basilica were used in the **Bishop's Palace** on Városház tér, which dates from 1801. A few metres south down Kossuth Lajos utca, the Baroque **St Stephen's Cathedral** dates in part from 1470, but has been modified on several occasions. The adjacent **Chapel of St Anna** was used by the Turks as a mosque until their exit from Székesfehérvár in 1688.

Back on Városház tér, the **City Hall** is a former palace dating from 1690; opposite, the **Franciscan Church and Monastery** has artwork depicting the life of Prince Imre. North along Fő utca, see some fine wood carvings in the **Cistercian Church** and the flower clock. An oddity in Székesfehérvár is **Bory Castle**, east of the centre at Máriavölgy utca 54. It evolved between 1923 and 1959 in Gothic, Romanesque and Scottish styles under the guidance of artist Jenő Bory and is filled with paintings and statues depicting his wife Ilona Komocsin.

WEDDING WATCH

Take a terrace table at the **Corvinus Restaurant** in **Sopron** on a sunny Saturday afternoon and watch the wedding parties coming and going across cobbled Fő tér to register at the Town Hall. Wedding couples and their entourages walk from the various churches in the town to sign the register and then pose for photographs before heading off across the square to their reception and making way for the next nuptial group – it makes a fascinating spectacle.

SOPRON

On a chunk of Hungarian territory jutting into Austria, Sopron proves a real find. This splendid town at the foot of the pine-clad Lővér Hills, with its subalpine climate, is packed with listed buildings – around 250 in all – with a preponderance of Gothic and early Baroque architecture reminiscent of Budapest's Castle District. Sopron has more **historical monuments** than any other Hungarian town and exploration of the Belváros (inner town) proves most rewarding.

The centre point of Sopron is delightful **Fő tér**, beneath the 60m (196ft) fire tower; from the tower, built on Roman foundations and completed in the late 17th century, trumpeters warned of fire and sounded the hours – climb it for a fine panorama of the place. By the tower, **Loyalty Gate** (1922) acknowledges the Sopron citizens' decision to choose Hungarian status after the Trianon Treaty of 1920; the Latin phrase *Civitas Fidelissima* on Sopron's coat of arms means 'most loyal citizenry'.

The Baroque **Holy Trinity Column** on Fő tér was completed in 1701. Behind it stands the **Goat Church**, so named after the heraldic identity of its main benefactor; here in the 17th century three coronations took place and the Hungarian parliament met several times. In a Gothic building next door is the **Pharmacy Museum**.

Along the square's northern side are Fabricius House at No. 6 and Storno House at No. 8, with the General's House between them. **Fabricius House** is a museum of 17th- and 18th-century Sopron domestic life, furnished

ISTVÁN THE GREAT

The mansion of one of Hungary's best-known families lies 13km (8 miles) southeast of Sopron. The neo-Classical **Széchenyi mansion**, just outside the village of **Nagycenk**, now contains an excellent museum showcasing the family. Notable achievements of Count István Széchenyi (1791–1860) – he was known as 'the greatest Hungarian' – included taming the Tisza River, increasing the Danube's navigability, helping to design the Chain Bridge, laying the foundations of Hungary's railway network, and introducing steamships to the Danube and Lake Balaton.

Opposite: *Floral spray decorates the bride's car for a wedding in Transdanubia.*
Left: *Esterházy Palace is the finest Baroque mansion in Hungary.*

accordingly; the Renaissance **Storno House** (1417) contains the worthwhile private art collection of the Storno dynasty; the **General's House** was the Mayor's residence in the 17th century.

From Fő tér, Templom utca and Új utca are parallel streets leading south. Templom utca contains more of Sopron's many museums – the **Mining Museum** in a former Esterházy mansion at No. 2, the **Forestry Museum** at No. 4, and the **Lutheran Museum** in the priests' seminary at No. 12, next to the **Lutheran Church** from 1782. On Új utca, a former Jewish street, are two 14th-century synagogues.

Esterházy Palace

Some 27km (16 miles) east of Sopron, **Fertőd** boasts Hungary's largest and most beautiful Baroque mansion. The 126-room Esterházy Palace, labelled the 'Hungarian Versailles', was started in 1720 and took 46 years to complete for the country's richest aristocratic family.

In its halcyon years during the latter part of the 18th century, and with **Joseph Haydn** as court composer, the palace cultivated a reputation for its sumptuous balls and social gatherings. But it fell into decline in the 1800s and only after World War II, when it served as a hospital, was restoration begun seriously. A tour of the palace takes in two dozen or so rooms; on summer weekends, concerts are staged here.

Opposite: *Sale time at a traditional costume shop in Szombathely.*
Right: *Kőszeg Town Hall bears an exterior collection of paintings.*

KŐSZEG

This small town at the foot of **Mount Írottkő**, at a height of 883m (2896ft) Transdanubia's tallest mountain, has a big claim to fame – the heroics of its people during a siege by the Turks in 1532, when local hero **Miklós Jurisics** and 400 men held out for 25 days against Suleiman's 100,000-strong army that was attempting to reach Vienna.

The **Kőszeg Castle** stronghold dates from the 13th century and now contains a small museum. Through **Heroes' Gate**, erected in 1932 on the siege's 400th anniversary, cobbled Jurisics tér displays a fine array of coloured buildings; they include the Gothic **Church of St James** (1407) containing Jurisics's tomb, the Baroque **Church of St Imre**, built for Lutherans, and the 14th-century largely Renaissance **Town Hall**. There are two pharmacy museums – the **Golden Unicorn** at No. 11 and the **Black Moor** at Rákóczi utca 3.

SZOMBATHELY

Founded as the Roman town of Savaria in AD43 on the Amber Route from the Baltic to the Mediterranean, Szombathely (the name means 'Saturday place' and refers to its medieval market) has important **Roman remains** in the **Romkert** (Garden of Ruins) behind the **Cathedral** and the **Iseum** (Temple of Isis) south of Fő tér. Next to the Iseum, the austere **Szombathely Gallery** is one of Hungary's leading modern art galleries.

The neo-Classical **Cathedral**, on Templom tér, was completed in 1815; its frescoes by Franz Anton Maulbertsch were lost in World War II bombing. However, the **Bishop's Palace** to its left, built around the same period, still has some fine 18th-century frescoes by István Dorffmeister in its ground-floor **Sala Terrena**.

BLOOD COUNTESS

The Nádasdy castle in Sárvár has ties with Hungary's most notorious woman of the 17th century – **Countess Erzsébet Báthory**. Known as the 'Blood Countess', she is said to have tortured and killed more than 600 women and girls while her husband, the 'Black Knight' **Ferenc Nádasdy**, was away fighting the Turks, and also after his death in 1604. After inheriting the Nádasdy estates, she was caught six years later and imprisoned in a Transylvanian castle, where she died in 1614.

At the far end of the building, the **Smidt Museum**, at Hollán Ernő utca 2, contains a fascinating miscellany of objects collected by Lajos Smidt.

Szombathely is frequented by Austrians who stream across the nearby border in search of bargain buys – and with good reason. Prices in Hungary are amazingly cheap by western European standards and Szombathely has a fine array of good quality but inexpensive clothes shops.

Above: *Sárvár Castle at the end of the footbridge.*
Opposite: *Exhibit at the Modern Hungarian Art Gallery in Pécs.*

SÁRVÁR

The name means 'mud castle', but that's history. The present castle in this spa town is 16th-century Renaissance, built for the **Nádasdy family** on the foundations of a medieval fort. Here the first Hungarian translation of the New Testament was printed in 1541. Accessed off Kossuth tér across a long brick footbridge, the castle contains outstanding ceiling frescoes in the **Knight's Hall** showing the Black Knight, Ferenc Nádasdy, fighting the Turks; biblical scenes by István Dorffmeister adorn the walls.

South of Sárvár and Szombathely, the forested **Őrség region** towards the Slovenian border contains delightful villages such as thatched **Őriszentpéter**, with its 13th-century Romanesque church, and **Szalafő**, the region's oldest settlement. There is a small Őrség *skansen* (folk museum) at nearby **Pityerszer**.

PÉCS

Tucked to the south of the Mecsek Hills, Pécs (pronounced 'Paich') is the focus of southern Transdanubia for the visitor: a centre for art and culture, reflected in its **museums** and **galleries**. The city had its origins with the Celts and Romans, when as Sophianae it was capital of Lower Pannonia. Made an episcopal seat by King Stephen in 1009, it became a **centre of learning** when Hungary's first university was established here in 1367.

INTO THE FOREST

The **Gemenc Forest**, 65km (40 miles) northeast of **Pécs**, is a 50,000ha (123,550-acre) protected landscape reserve where backwaters, oxbow lakes, ponds and islands cover the Danube's former floodplain; the great river was straightened around a century ago to stop flooding. The reserve, with its willow, oak and poplar trees, now supports birds such as herons, white-tailed eagles, black storks and tufted herons, as well as all manner of animals – deer, boar and wildcat among them. It is possible to visit the forest by narrow-gauge train, on horseback or by boat – but not on foot.

Captured by the Turks in 1543, Pécs underwent dramatic change until their eviction in 1686. The city's recovery was slow, but it was aided by a revival in **wine** production and the discovery of **coal** that provided a springboard to industry.

Pécs's past is characterized by the former **Mosque of Pasha Gazi Kasim** on Széchenyi tér – it is Hungary's largest Turkish building and now a **Catholic church**. On the north side of the square, with the **Trinity Column** (1908) at its centre, the **Archaeology Museum** plots the region's pre-Magyar evolution.

A block further north, museums on Káptalan utca compete for attention. The **Zsolnay Porcelain Museum** is at No. 2, and across the street at No. 3 is the **Vasarely Museum** with op art canvases by world-renowned Viktor Vasarely who was born in the house in 1908; here, too, is a **Mining Museum**. The **Modern Hungarian Art Gallery**, exhibiting 19th- and 20th-century fine art, occupies No. 4; work by artists Endre Nemes and Erzsébet Schaár fills No. 5; and work by non-figurative painter and sculptor Ferenc Martyn is in No. 6.

Continue further and you will eventually emerge on Dóm tér, where the four-towered **St Peter's Basilica** has been rebuilt several times since the 11th-century original; the latest exterior guise is neo-Romanesque. To your left facing the basilica is the neo-Renaissance **Bishop's Palace**, from the 1770s; the unusual modern statue on a balcony is of Franz Liszt. Below the basilica on Janus Pannonius utca is the **Csontváry Museum** (*see* panel, page 39).

A FINE VINTAGE

The seven hills that surround the ancient town of **Szekszárd** produce some of Hungary's finest red wine. The town itself is almost 1000 years old, and there were vineyards here long before that in Roman times. Serious wine production started in the 18th century and much was exported – to Britain among other countries. Composers **Liszt**, who often visited Szekszárd, and **Schubert** were said to be enthusiastic drinkers of the town's tipple.

VILLAGE MUSEUM

The village of **Szenna**, 9km (6 miles) southwest of Kaposvár, has one of the best (though smallest) *skanzens*, or **open-air museums**, in Hungary. It consists of six traditional **farmhouses** from the local Zselic area rebuilt around an 18th-century **Calvinist church**, giving the 'village' an authentic feel. The church, which boasts a fine painted and coffered wooden ceiling, is still used for worship.

Below: *Széchenyi tér in Pécs, with the Trinity Column and Mosque Church of the Turks.*

AROUND PÉCS

Mohács, southeast of Pécs, was the scene of Hungary's defeat by the Turks on 29 August 1526 that cost the lives of 20,000 men; the disaster was followed by more than 150 years of Turkish rule and a prolonged loss of Hungarian independence. The **battlefield site** is 7km (4 miles) south of the town; in town two branches of the **Dorottya Kanizsai Museum** (at Városház utca 1 and Szerb utca 2) recount the conflict. The **Votive Church** on Széchenyi tér was built in 1926, the battle's 400th anniversary year.

South of Pécs, **Siklós** is famed for its **castle**, though its origins are obscure. The main building is 18th-century Baroque; the surrounds date from the 15th century and the foundations were laid at least two centuries earlier. Northeast of Pécs, the **castle** at **Pécsvárad** was built in the 13th century on an earlier Benedictine monastery founded by King Stephen.

Between Mohács and Siklós, **Villány** sits among vineyards that produce full-bodied red wines – sample them at the **Wine Museum** and in a row of protected cellars on the Pécs road at **Villánykövesd**.

Transdanubia at a Glance

Transdanubia is best in **summer**, though the weather is good from May to October.

There are good **rail** and **bus** connections from Budapest.

Buses link the towns of Transdanubia, from Győr to Pécs. **Trains** are also an option.

MID-RANGE

Club Hotel Aranysárkány, Rákóczi út 120, Kőszeg, tel: 94 364 122; fax: 94 362 296. Fine three-star, 15 minutes from Kőszeg's historic centre.
Danubius Thermal Hotel Sárvár, Rákóczi Ferenc utca 1, 9600 Sárvár, tel: 95 323 999; fax: 95 320 406. Spa hotel with thermal baths.
Főnix, Hunyadi János út 2, 7621 Pécs, tel: 72 311 680; fax: 72 324 113. Two-star near museums and cathedral.
Fonte, Schweidel utca 17, 9022 Győr, tel: 96 513 810; fax: 96 513 820. Pretty three-star panzió opposite the National Theatre.
Klastrom, Zechmeister utca 1, 9021 Győr, tel: 96 315 611; fax: 96 327 030. Three-star in 250-year-old former convent; the chestnut tree in the yard is even older.
Palatinus, Új utca 23, 9400 Sopron, tel: 99 523 610; fax: 99 311 395. Three-star hotel located in Sopron's old town.

Palatinus, Király utca 5, 7621 Pécs, tel: 72 233 022; fax: 72 232 261. Art Deco hotel in mid-town, has a bowling alley.
Savaria, Mártirók tere 4, 9700 Szombathely, tel: 94 311 440; fax: 94 324 532. Art Nouveau creation of 1917; its chandeliered restaurant is grand.
Wollner, Templom utca 20, 9400 Sopron, tel: 99 524 400; fax: 99 326 735. Small three-star in 300-year-old palace; large garden, wine cellar.

MID-RANGE

Bécsikapu, Rajnis utca 5, Kőszeg, tel: 30 937 7799. Ten soups and more on the extensive Hungarian menu.
Cézár Pince, Hátsókapu utca 2, Sopron, tel: 99 311 337. One of the best venues in town, in a medieval wine cellar on the corner of Orsolya tér.
Kreszta-Ház, Jedlik Anyos utca 3, Gyòr, tel: 96 318 435, 96 315 744. Italian, Russian, Mexican ... Hungarian even, in the old part of Győr.
Ferencesek Vendéglo, Ferencesek utcáya 24, 7621 Pécs, tel: 72 325 239. Homely Hungarian dishes; quiet street.

Fortuna Internet Café, Ferencesek utcáya 32, 7621 Pécs, tel: 72 332 150. Has a restaurant and beer garden.
Pannónia Étterem, Fő tér 29, Szombathely, tel: 94 509 588. Hungarian menu. Prints of old Szombathely on the walls.
Várkapu, Várkerület 5, 9600 Sárvár, tel: 95 320 475. Offers a vegetarian selection.

In Győr, **Ciklámen Tourist**, at Aradi vértanúk útja 22 (tel: 96 311 557) arranges tours to Pannonhalma, Sopron and the Esterházy Palace at Fertőd. In Pécs, **Mecsek Tours**, at Széchenyi tér 1 (tel: 72 212 044) covers Mohács and other areas of southern Transdanubia.

Tourinform offices at Győr (Árpád utca 32, 9021 Győr, tel: 96 317 709, written and phone inquiries only); Sopron (Előkapu utca 11, 9400 Sopron, tel: 99 338 592); Székesfehérvár (Városház tér 1, 8000 Székesfehérvár, tel: 22 312 818); and Pécs (Széchenyi tér 9, 7621 Pécs, tel: 72 213 315).

PÉCS	J	F	M	A	M	J	J	A	S	O	N	D
AVERAGE TEMP. °F	32	35	44	51	60	65	69	69	63	53	41	35
AVERAGE TEMP. °C	0	1	6	10	15	18	20	20	17	11	5	1
HOURS OF SUN DAILY	2	3	5	6	8	9	10	10	9	7	4	2
RAINFALL in	1.5	1.5	1.4	2.2	2.5	3.3	2.6	2.4	1.9	1.5	2.2	1.9
RAINFALL mm	38.1	38.1	35.6	55.9	63.5	83.8	66	61	48.3	38.1	55.9	48.3
DAYS OF RAINFALL	11	11	10	12	12	13	12	12	11	11	11	10

6
The Great Plain

Everyone knows about Hungary's Great Plain, that huge untamed land of mirages, endless grasslands and far distant horizons that, at an area of 45,000km² (17,370 sq miles), constitutes almost half of the country's territory. The **Danube River** divides Hungary in two; the eastern half of the country is further split by the **Tisza River**, which flows southwards across the dried-up bed of a former inland sea.

It may be rather flat, but the *puszta* – Hungary's very own prairie – is certainly by no means boring. In **Debrecen** and **Szeged**, it has two cities that vie for the title 'King of the Plain'. There are also other interesting places to visit, like **Kecskemét** and **Szolnok**, as well as countless small towns and villages and scattered white-walled farmsteads, known as *tanyák*.

The traditional images that most people have of the Great Plain – a romantic part of the country known as **Alföld** to Hungarians – are of shepherds braving the worst of the winter weather to tend their long-horned flock, and of horseherds riding brazenly at high speed across the flat grassy lands in summer.

There is another image, though, for which the Great Plain is known – the natural phenomenon of the *délibáb*, where an inverted **mirage** of a distant village floats above the horizon. As you gaze upon the grazing cattle and the thatched *csárdák* (village inns), you become aware that life on the Great Plain has changed very little down the centuries, and also appears unlikely to alter much in the future.

DON'T MISS

** **Kalocsa:** visit Hungary's paprika capital.
** **Hortobágy:** home to the Máta stud farm.
** **Kecskemét:** colourful Art Nouveau buildings.
** **Jászberény:** visit the Jász Museum, which houses the famous Lehel Horn.
* **Debrecen:** explore the Déri Museum of *puszta* life.
* **Szeged:** see the splendid New Synagogue in the Jewish quarter.
* **Kiskunság National Park:** a UNESCO bioreserve.

Opposite: *Kecskemét's tiled Ornamental Palace is the pick of its Art Nouveau buildings.*

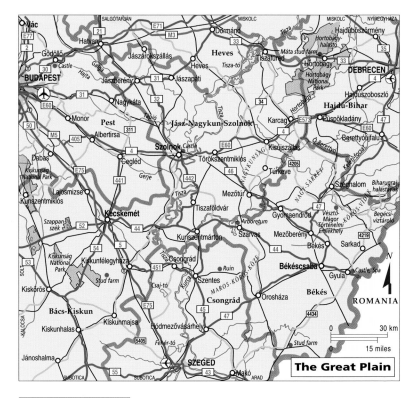

The Great Plain

THE EASTERN PLAIN
Debrecen

Debrecen is the second-largest city in Hungary, a seat
of learning since the Middle Ages that briefly became
the seat of government during the 1848–49 **War of
Independence**. It was known as the 'Calvinist Rome' in
the 16th century, and the mighty, yellow, neo-Classical
Calvinist **Great Church** that dominates Kossuth tér is
today very much the symbol of the city.

The church, which can hold up to 3000 people, was
designed by Mihály Pollack and contains the armchair
from which Lajos Kossuth read the declaration of independence from the Habsburgs on 14 April 1849; here,
too, is Hungary's largest **bell** and a splendid **organ**.

Behind the church, on Kalvin tér, is the **Calvinist College**, founded as a theological institute in the 16th century. The present enlarged version dates from 1816 and contains a **library** with more than 600,000 volumes, and the **oratory** where the National Assembly met in 1849.

The best museum in Debrecen is the **Déri Museum**, housing a detailed display of *puszta* life and, in a separate gallery, a treasured trilogy of works by the noted Hungarian painter Mihály Munkácsy (1844–1900) – *Pilate Before Christ*, the dramatic *Ecce Homo*, and *Golgotha*.

Also worth a look in Debrecen's compact centre are the impressive neo-Classical **City Hall** on Piac utca; the Calvinist **Small Church**, minus its onion dome lost in a storm in 1909, on Révész tér; the early 20th-century **Status Que Synagogue** on Kápolnási utca; and the Baroque (and formerly Piarist) **St Anna's Church** on Szent Anna utca. The **windmill** at Böszörményi út, northwest of the centre, is said to the largest of its kind in central Europe.

If you are in Debrecen in summer, you might catch the four-day **Flower Carnival** which culminates on 20 August with a procession and firework display. In March the **Spring Festival** is a showcase for music and drama and **Jazz Days** attracts Hungarian and international performers.

> **THE CALVINISTS**
>
> The Calvinist faith that spread through Hungary in the mid-16th century – named after its founder, Geneva priest **John Calvin** (1509–64) – found a base in **Debrecen** after its followers had made a deal with the occupying Turks that ensured their safety. In 1674, the Catholic **Habsburgs** deported 41 Calvinist ministers from Debrecen to become galley slaves; they are remembered on a memorial erected in 1895, at which **Pope John Paul II** placed a wreath in 1991 as a gesture of reconciliation.

Hortobágy

The 700km^2 (270 sq miles) of **Hortobágy National Park**, set aside in 1973, make up one of Europe's largest protected grasslands. Located northwest of Debrecen, this is where the romantic ideal of the *puszta* is played out to the full. Here you will find grey long-horned cattle and flocks of *racka* sheep with their distinctive corkscrew horns. There is a wide variety of bird life in the park too – from eagles and cranes to herons and storks.

Below: *A glimpse of past rural life in the museum at Hortobágy.*

The composer Zoltán Kodály (1882–1967), who lived and worked in **Kecskemét**, is known for his revolutionary and inspirational way of teaching – the **Kodály Method**, based on use of the human voice, which is now practised in Hungary and throughout the world. With **Béla Bartók** he closely studied **Hungarian folk music**, blending its traditional forms into compositions of his own, such as *Peacock Variations*. Students from all over the world follow his methods at the **Kodály Institute** in Kecskemét.

Opposite: *Traditional Hungarian gypsy ensemble playing the music of the Great Plain.*
Below: *The stately Katona Theatre in Kecskemét pays tribute to the town's romantic playwright.*

The landmark nine-arched **bridge** across the Hortobágy River dates from 1833; next to it is the thatched **Hortobágy Csárda**, now much restored. The **Shepherds' Museum** on Petőfi tér shows how the men of the plain lived, worked and dressed, with fine examples of their embroidered capes, or *szűr*. The **Hortobágy Gallery** in the old town hall displays pictures with a *puszta* theme. Across the bridge a couple of kilometres north of Hortobágy village is the `Máta stud farm`, where you can take a carriage tour, watch equestrian displays and have riding lessons.

THE SOUTHERN PLAIN
Kecskemét

An impressive blend of Baroque, Art Nouveau and contemporary buildings fill the streets around the leafy swathe that forms the centrepiece of Kecskemét, a lovely town on the fringe of the southern Great Plain.

According to Brahms, Kecskemét was the 'most beautiful town in the world'. Though the Ottomans wrought havoc across the Great Plain for 150 years, Kecskemét was spared their excesses and came to be ruled directly by the sultan – hence its development as a centre for the **arts** and **education**.

The vineyards and apricot orchards that start where the town ends give Kecskemét its garden city character.

The **vines**, planted in the 19th century to bind the sandy soil, are today responsible for a third of Hungary's wine production; the **apricots** are used to make the region's famous apricot brandy, *barackpálinka*.

The centre of Kecskemét is based on two large open squares, Szabadság tér and Kossuth tér, which join in a single expanse of inner-city

JÓZSEF KATONA

The **Katona Theatre** in Kecskemét, built in 1896 on the lines of the Vígszínház in Budapest, is named after the town's playwright son József Katona (1791–1830), whose best-known work, **Bánk Bán**, was made into a successful opera by Ferenc Erkel. The **Katona Museum** at Katona József utca 5 is dedicated to his memory. Outside the town hall, a memorial marks the spot where he died.

greenery. On the north side of Szabadság tér you can't miss the distinctive **Cifrapalota** (Ornamental Palace), a remarkable piece of Art Nouveau complete with glazed majolica tiles built in 1902. It now houses the **Kecskemét Gallery**, and upstairs is a fine tile-decorated hall that was once a casino.

Facing the square across the twin-carriageway Rákóczi utca is the white Moorish-Romantic-style former **Synagogue**, completed in 1871; it is now the **House of Science and Technology** exhibition venue. On the east side of the square opposite the Cifrapalota is the **New College**, built in the Gothic style of Transylvania (1912), which now houses the **Ecclesiastical Art Collection**.

The **Calvinist Church** on the east side of Kossuth tér is from the 17th century; the **Franciscan Church** just south of it has 13th-century origins. Behind the Franciscan Church, the **Kodály Institute** (*see* panel opposite) occupies the Baroque former Franciscan monastery. The square's south side is taken up by Ödön Lechner's grand pink **Town Hall** (1893) and the Baroque Catholic **Great Church** (1806).

Diverse museums in Kecskemét include the **Hungarian Photography Museum** (Bajcsy-Zsilinszky utca) with some 300,000 photos; the **Naive Art Museum** (Gáspár András utca) and nearby **Toy Museum**, the **Hungarian Folk Craft Museum** (Serföző utca), and the **Musical Instrument Museum** (Zimay utca).

SAUSAGE TOWN

Békéscsaba (pop. 70,000) in southeastern Hungary has a tasty claim to fame – as the country's 'sausage capital', where several varieties are produced. The **Csaba Sausage Festival** in late October, in which 100 teams take part in a sausage-making competition, is a celebration with music and dancing of Békéscsaba's dedication to the sausage – the festival is named after a locally produced salami. Szeged has its own Pick salami, a smoked pork product named after a 19th-century local butcher.

Above: *Paprika and garlic are key ingredients of Hungarian cuisine.*

To the south of Kecskemét, the 11,000ha (27,181-acre) Bugacpuszta is the most accessible section of **Kiskunság National Park**, a 35,000ha (86,485-acre) UNESCO bioreserve. In the tourism centre close to Bugac village, equestrian displays include dressage and carriage driving. The **Herders' Museum** shows the everyday life of the shepherd.

If you missed out on the paprika and embroidery sold and displayed at Tihany on Lake Balaton, don't despair. **Kalocsa**, some 120km (80 miles) due south of Budapest, is Hungary's paprika capital with an abundance of the 'red gold'. The **Paprika Museum** and **Károly Viski Museum** with its folk costume collection, both on Szent István király út, are worth a look.

Szeged

Like Kalocsa, Szeged on the River Tisza is heavily into **paprika** production. Rivalling Debrecen as the most important city on the Great Plain, the city of 185,000 people bears a name derived from *sziget*, or island; with 2100 hours of sun a year it is also dubbed 'the sunshine town'.

Precious little of early Szeged remains. Though its trading origins go back to the 13th century and, like Kecskemét, the city was afforded protection under the Turks, all but 300 of its buildings were destroyed in a single night during the **great flood** of March 1879.

The city was rebuilt between 1880 and 1883 with funding from foreign capitals that gave their name to sections of the outer ring road – London, Berlin, Paris, Brussels and others – and new buildings emerged in a range of styles. In 1956, Szeged was the scene of a **student uprising** that predated that of Budapest.

SUICIDE TOWN

Hungary has the worst suicide record in Europe and one of the worst in the world, at around 40 per 100,000 head of population. **Csongrád**, 50km (30 miles) southeast of Kecskemét, is credited with heading Hungary's suicide statistics. Psychologists seeking an answer say it is possibly precipitated by the recurring harshness of winter on the Great Plain.

Szeged is a city of two squares – **Dom tér**, edged with some of the city's finest buildings, and leafy **Széchenyi tér**, containing the neo-Baroque **Town Hall** with its Venice-style 'Bridge of Sighs', fountains and statues. Towards the river are the neo-Classical **Ferenc Móra Museum** on Roosevelt tér, including an exhibit of 7th-century Avar culture, and the **Castle Museum** within the castle ruins.

Dom tér is the larger of the squares, bordered by statues of Hungarian worthies. It is dominated by the huge brown brick neo-Romanesque **Votive Church** (1930) with its 10,000-pipe organ; the church's construction was funded by survivors of the flood. The octagonal **Demetrius Tower** close by is all that is left of a 13th-century church. In the square's northeast corner, the **Serbian Orthodox Church** has a fine Rococo iconostasis with pear-wood surrounds.

Szeged's **Jewish quarter**, just west of the centre on Jósika utca, is centred on the **New Synagogue**, a Moorish Art Nouveau building from 1903 that is among Europe's finest Jewish places of worship. The white, blue and gold interior, topped by a blue glass cupola representing the universe, is most impressive.

> ### TISZA'S RESORT
>
> The damming of the Tisza River 70km (43 miles) west of Debrecen to create a reservoir gave rise to the area's first resort on the new Lake Tisza. **Tiszafüred**, a quiet town on the Tisza River until the early 1980s, now welcomes holidaymaking families to its sandy strand and thermal bath – also for boating and fishing. The **Pál Kiss Museum**, set up in a 19th-century manor house in 1949, was Hungary's first village museum; it contains good local ceramics.

Gyula

Almost on the Romanian border, lively Gyula is an attractive **spa town** with parks, gardens and a 15th-century **Gothic castle**, the only intact brick castle in this part of Europe – its courtyard is the setting for historical drama performances in summer. The **Várfürdő** (Castle Baths) complex contains 20 thermal indoor and outdoor pools.

Ferenc Erkel (1810–93), composer of Hungary's national anthem, was born in Gyula and his house (Apor Vilmos tér 7) is now a **museum** devoted to his life – items on view include a harmonium, music scores and family photos. The **Ladics House** (Jókai Mór utca 4) is a superbly furnished 19th-century bourgeois family home.

Below: *One of the four largest rivers in Hungary, the Tisza, stretching 598km (372 miles).*

Szarvas, situated more or less midway between Gyula and Kecskemét, is known for its 82ha (203-acre) **arboretum**, the best in Hungary and in part laid out on the lines of Vienna's Schönbrunn Palace gardens. It contains more than 1500 different species of trees and shrubs.

Above: *Riverside gardens in Szolnok – the town grew up at a crossing point of the Tisza River.*

THE CENTRAL PLAIN
Szolnok

At the confluence of the Tisza and its Zagyva tributary, Szolnok – home to 80,000 people – is the most important town on the Central Plain and a pleasant point to break a journey to the eastern part of the country. Its strategic site as a crossing point of the Tisza made it vulnerable to attack down the centuries – from the Mongols in the 13th century to the advancing Soviet troops, Allied bombing and fleeing Nazis in World War II.

Szolnok's **castle**, founded in 1506, was destroyed by the Habsburgs two centuries later – all that remains is a chunk of wall by the **artists' colony** on Gutenberg tér, across the Zagyva River from the town. Other finds from earlier times, along with work of the artists' colony, are displayed in the **János Damjanich Museum** (Kossuth tér 4), named after the victorious general at the battle of Szolnok in 1849.

Some 50km (30 miles) east of Budapest, a number of towns and villages prefixed 'Jász-' have links with the Jazygian ethnic group who arrived from the region of the Caspian Sea in the 13th century. Chief among them is **Jászberény**, where the **Jász Museum** houses the **Lehel Horn** – a beautifully carved Byzantine ivory horn with which the Magyar leader Lehel is said to have killed his captor, the German emperor Otto I, at the Battle of Augsburg in AD955.

BLACK POTTERY

They have been making the distinctive black pottery associated with the small town of **Nádudvar**, west of Debrecen, for more than two centuries. The decorated jugs, vases and candlesticks are smoked and polished rather than glazed, making them instantly recognizable. The craft, which has been handed down through successive generations of the Fazekas family, can be witnessed in the pottery workshop of **Lajos Fazekas** at Fő utca 159.

The Great Plain at a Glance

Winter is usually cold and windy. The long **summer** days let you make the most of the plain, though late **spring** and early **autumn** are also good.

Intercity **trains** connect Budapest to Debrecen, Békéscsaba, Kecskemét, Szolnok and Szeged. **Buses** link the capital with Kalocsa.

Direct **rail** and **bus** services get you around. The main transport hubs are Debrecen and Szeged, which can be reached on cross-border rail services from neighbouring countries.

Mid-range
Aranyhomok, Széchenyi tér 2, 6000 Kecskemét, tel: 76 486 286. The 'Golden Sands', Kecskemét's largest hotel, is very central, on Kossuth tér.
Beta Hotel Kalocsa, Szentháromság tér 4, 6300 Kalocsa, tel/fax: 78 461 244. Three-star with 29 rooms in 200-year-old building.
Grand Hotel Aranybika, Piac utca 11–15, 4024 Debrecen, tel: 52 416 777. The 'Golden Bull' (1690) claims to be the ciountry's oldest hotel; visitors may choose between the historic part or the modern wing.
Hungária, Maros utca 2, 6720 Szeged, tel: 62 480 580. Three-star, one of Szeged's oldest, with fine river views.

Royal, Kolcsey utca 1, 6720 Szeged, tel: 62 475 275. Long-established hotel with 110 rooms, in the centre of town.
Tisza, Verseghy Park 2, 5000 Szolnok, tel: 56 371 155; fax: 56 421 520. This grand 33-room hotel (built in 1928) has its own thermal bath (closed in midsummer), as well as a pub and lots of atmosphere.

Mid-range
Civis Hotel, Kálvin tér 4, 4024 Debrecen, tel: 52 418 522. Smart hotel restaurant, rated as being one of Debrecen's most popular dining venues.
Liberté, Szabadság tér 2, Kecskemét, tel: 76 328 636. Goose liver omelette, steaks. Elegant terrace restaurant on Kecskemét's main square.
Royal Hotel, Kolcsey utca 1, 6720 Szeged, tel: 62 475 275. Beautiful hotel restaurant offering a wide choice of traditional Hungarian dishes. There is also live gypsy music.
Tisza Hotel, Verseghy Park 2, 5000 Szolnok, tel: 56 371 155. Hotel restaurant with riverside garden is the pick of a limited restaurant choice in Szolnok.

In Debrecen, **Hajdútourist**, at Kálvin tér 2 (tel: 52 415 588), includes city-related tours and *puszta* excursions to Hortobágy.
In Szeged, **Szeged Tourist**, at Klauzál tér 2 (tel: 62 321 800), offers excursions which include city sightseeing as well as Tisza boat trips.
In Kecskemét, **Piroska Tours**, at Szabadság tér 2 (tel: 76 328 636), includes equestrian shows in its tour programme.

For further information about what is on offer in the Great Plain, contact **Tourinform** offices at Debrecen (Piac utca 20, 4024 Debrecen, tel: 52 412 250); Gyula (Kossuth Lajos utca 7, 5700 Gyula, tel: 66 463 421); Kecskemét (Kossuth tér 1, 6000 Kecskemét, tel: 76 481 065); Szeged (Victor Hugo utca 1, 6720 Szeged, tel: 62 311 711); Szolnok (Ságvári körút 4, 5000 Szolnok, tel: 56 424 803); and Tiszafüred (Húszöles utca 21, 5350 Tiszafüred, tel: 59 353 000).

DEBRECEN	J	F	M	A	M	J	J	A	S	O	N	D
AVERAGE TEMP. °F	27	32	41	52	60	67	70	69	62	51	42	33
AVERAGE TEMP. °C	-3	0	5	11	16	19	21	21	17	11	6	1
HOURS OF SUN DAILY	2	3	5	6	8	9	10	9	7	5	2	2
RAINFALL in	1.3	1.4	1.2	1.5	2.4	3.2	2.2	2.5	1.6	1.9	2.1	1.5
RAINFALL mm	34	35	30	37	60	80	56	64	40	49	53	39
DAYS OF RAINFALL	13	11	11	11	13	13	11	10	8	10	12	13

7
Northern Hungary

Northern Hungary – northeast from Budapest along the Slovak border – is **hill territory**, much of it forested. From the Börzsöny Hills of the Danube Bend, the Carpathian foothills extend some 260km (162 miles), embracing the Cserhát, Mátra, Bükk, Aggtelek and Zemplén hill ranges. The highest summits in Hungary are in the Mátra Hills – **Kékestető** at 1014m (3327ft) and **Galyatető** at 965m (3162ft). The volcanic Mátra Hills, 80km (50 miles) from Budapest, are the most accessible uplands for the capital's dwellers. Mount Kékestető even lends itself to winter sports, offering a pair of ski runs.

Impressive cave systems exist beneath the limestone landscape of **Aggtelek National Park** that forms the border with Slovakia, a protected area given UNESCO World Heritage status in 1985. Some of the caves remain unexplored; others provided shelter for Neolithic man. There are 700 caves in all, many with characteristic stalactites and stalagmites and the larger number on the Slovakian side.

The **Bükk Hills** are best visited in autumn, when the leaves on the beech trees turn a burnished gold. A large tract of the region has been turned into a National Park, home to the famous Lippizaner horses; bird and wildlife proliferates in the region, which provides a scenic backdrop for the cities of Eger and Miskolc.

Driving around this part of Hungary is sheer pleasure, through rural communities where cars have yet to find a place and along lanes populated only by slow-moving farm trailers. Take your time getting about the region – as everyone else does.

DON'T MISS

** Eger: known for its castle and fine Baroque architecture.
** Hollókő: quintessential picture-postcard folk village.
** Szilvásvárad: visit the breeding centre and see the Lippizaner horses.
** Aggtelek National Park: explore the park's fascinating stalactite cave system.
* Tokaj: centre of Hungary's famous wine region.
* Bükk National Park: the ideal spot for hiking.
* Gyöngyös: of interest is the natural history section of the Mátra Museum.

Opposite: *Eger is well-known for its impressive Baroque architecture.*

PALÓC PEOPLE

Visit **Hollókő** in summer and you will almost certainly see women wearing traditional embroidered Palóc costume for the benefit of tourists. The Palóc are an ethnic grouping who originated in what is present-day **Slovakia** and they live mostly in the **Cserhát Hills** towards the Slovak border. As well as keeping alive Hungarian folk traditions, the Palóc are known for their dialect – a rarity in Hungary. **Balassagyarmat**, the 'Palóc capital', tells their story in the **Palóc Museum**.

GÖDÖLLŐ

Gödöllő, at the end of the HÉV line from Budapest, is where you'll find the **Grassalkovich Palace,** the former summer residence of the **Habsburgs** – in its day it was equally as impressive as the Esterházy Palace in northern Transdanubia. The palace was designed by András Mayerhoffer in the 1740s; in the 19th century, it was a favourite residence of **Emperor Franz Josef** and his wife **Elizabeth** (Sissy). However, it fell into decay during the two World Wars and restoration only began in the early 1990s. The state rooms and several of the other rooms are now open for public inspection.

HOLLÓKŐ

Hollókő is Hungary's ultimate picture-postcard village, its two parallel streets of traditional whitewashed **Palóc houses** and discreet souvenir shops attracting thousands of visitors each year. The houses look older than they are; the entire village centre of 65 houses, tucked beneath the 13th-century hilltop **castle**, was rebuilt in medieval style after a fire in 1909. You may catch sight of a local woman wearing the colourful embroidered Palóc dress.

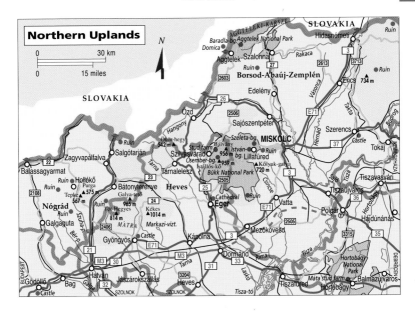

The village, about 17km (11 miles) southeast of Szécsény in the Cserhát Hills, was added to UNESCO's **World Heritage List** in 1987.

GYÖNGYÖS

Gateway to the **Mátra Hills**, Gyöngyös claims to have Hungary's largest Gothic church – **St Bartholomew's**, built in the 14th century but extensively remodelled in Baroque style four centuries later. The town is also home to the **Mátra Museum** (Kossuth Lajos utca 40), where exhibits of the region's natural history include a complete mammoth skeleton and what is claimed to be Europe's largest collection of birds' eggs.

EGER

Eger is known mainly for its splendid Baroque architecture, the **castle** and excellent **Egri Bikavér**, a tipple known the world over as Bull's Blood.

Historically, Eger's greatest moment came in 1552, when just 2000 Hungarian militia under István Dobó

Opposite: *The church and traditional Palóc houses in Hollókő, a pretty village in Northern Hungary.*

Above: *Eger's castle stands proud above the appealing city.*

successfully defended the castle against some 40,000 marauding Turks; legend has it that the resourceful womenfolk played their part by dousing the invaders with hot soup. However, in 1596, the Turks returned to take the city and stayed for 100 years; the 40m (131ft) **minaret** that rises above Eger's rooftops is their legacy (climb its 100 steps for a city overview). Within the castle are the remains of the 12th-century **St John's Cathedral**.

The present-day **Eger Cathedral**, completed in 1836, is Hungary's second largest church after the Esztergom basilica and bears a strong resemblance to it – both neo-Classical buildings were designed by József Hild. Its **organ** is the largest in the land. Next to it, the rambling Baroque **Archbishop's Palace** has been home to Eger's bishops for 250 years. Across the square, the late 18th-century Baroque **Lyceum** – now a teachers' training college – contains a couple of real gems in its stunning first-floor **Diocesan Library** and sixth-floor **observatory**, complete with a 200-year-old camera obscura.

Other Eger highlights include the **Cistercian Church** on Széchenyi István utca (1743), the exquisite twin-

towered Baroque **Minorite Church** on Dobó István tér
(1773) and, on Kossuth Lajos utca, the **Franciscan Church**
(1755) and **County Hall**, with its impressive wrought-
iron work by Henrik Fazola.

Eger is situated between the Mátra Hills to the west
and Bükk Hills stretching northeast towards Miskolc;
the limestone Bükk Hills take their name from the covering beech trees and now constitute **Bükk National
Park**. In their midst, the **Szalajka Valley** is a noted
place of beauty – its **Forestry Museum** dwells on the
life and times of the charcoal burners and foresters
hereabouts.

At **Szilvásvárad**, 27km (17 miles) north of Eger, the
estate of the pro-Fascist Pallavicinis is now a breeding
centre for the famous Lippizaner horses (*see* panel, page
118). In **Mezőkövesd**, 18km (11 miles) southeast of Eger,
the culture of the local Mátyó people – known for their
exquisite rose embroidery – come under scrutiny in the
Mátyó Museum.

MISKOLC

Miskolc is Hungary's third-largest city (after Budapest
and Debrecen), but its concentration of **industry** tends
to deter visitors. The **Orthodox Church**, with its impressive 16m (52ft) high iconostasis depicting Jesus's
life in 88 scenes, is one good reason to go; another is
the **Black Madonna of
Kazan** icon which was
given to the church by
Catherine the Great. The
**Hungarian Orthodox
Ecclesiastical Museum**
has Hungary's richest
Orthodox collection.

Below: *Miskolc is
Hungary's third largest
city, its industrial heritage
very much to the fore.*

Lillafüred, about 12km
(8 miles) west of Miskolc,
can be reached by narrow-
gauge train. It is a
peaceful spot dominated
by the grand **Palota Hotel**,

built in Gothic style near Lake Hámor in 1927. Three limestone caves are worth exploration – **Anna Cave**, which is near the hotel; the stalactite cave of **St Stephen**; and **Szeleta Cave** above the Miskolc road. Some 60km (40 miles) to the north is **Aggtelek National Park**, a UNESCO World Heritage Site where the **Baradla– Domica** cave network includes Europe's largest stalactite system.

Above: *Flower-decked balcony above the main street in Tokaj.*

TOKAJ

Tokaj is the hub of the prestigious **Tokaj–Hegyalja wine-growing region** on the edge of the Zemplén Hills, stretching alongside the Bodrog River. The region's wines are legion (*see* panel, this page) and there are cellars in Tokaj and its surrounds where you can duly pass judgement; the best-known is **Rákóczi Pince**, at Kossuth tér 15. The **Tokaj Museum**, at Bethlen Gábor utca 7, tells all you need to know of the region's viniculture.

Some 20km (12 miles) west of Tokaj is **Szerencs**, 'the gate of Hegyalja', where the **Zemplén Museum** collection is housed in a 16th-century Renaissance mansion. It includes the world's third-largest postcard collection – 825,000 cards in all. For those with a sweet tooth, the **Sugar Museum** has exhibits from 50 countries. Also worth a close look is **Sárospatak**, towards the Slovak border, where the Renaissance **castle** – one of the best examples of its kind in Hungary – was the domain of the Rákóczi family until 1711, when the failure of Ferenc Rákóczi II against the Habsburgs forced him into exile in Turkey. The town's renowned **Calvinist College** was founded in 1531; visitors can look over the college's **Great Library** with its 75,000 volumes.

Northern Hungary at a Glance

The towns and villages of Northern Hungary are at their best in **summer**. The hills of the region make good hiking from late **spring** through to early **autumn**, when the changing colours add that extra dimension.

There are half a dozen through **trains** daily from Budapest to Eger; otherwise you change at Füzesabony, on the Budapest-Miskolc line. Miskolc has international rail connections into Poland and Slovakia. **Bus** connections from Budapest are good.

Bus services within Northern Hungary are more than adequate, with regular departures from Eger and Miskolc to most points. **Trains** serve many places, including Tokaj.

MID-RANGE
Castlehotel Sasvár, Kossuth utca 1, 3242 Parádsasvár, tel/fax: 36 444 444. Five-star Neo-Renaissance manor house with 60 guest rooms, designed by Miklós Ybl in 1882 for Count György Károlyi.
Offi-ház, Dobó István tér 5, 3300 Eger, tel/fax: 36 311 005, 36 311 330. Eger's master confectioner Lajos Kopcsik created the Buona-

Offenbacher family's sugared coat of arms up the stairs in this centrally located three-star hotel.
Palota, Vadas Jenő utca, Lillafüred, tel: 46 331 411. Mock Gothic hotel with a beautiful terraced garden, situated in a large park close to the shore of Lake Hámor – it was once a trade union holiday home.
Pannonia, Kossuth Lajos utca 2, 3530 Miskolc, tel: 46 329 811. This centrally located 34-room upmarket hotel is rated as being among the best accommodation in town.
Senator-ház, Dobó István tér 11, 3300 Eger, tel/fax: 36 320 466. By common consent, this is the best place in town. The 18th-century inn has only 11 rooms, so early booking is advised.
Szent János, Szent János utca 3, 3300 Eger, tel: 36 410 409; fax: 36 312 164. Centrally placed, airy and modern three-star with aerobics classes before breakfast if you care to join in.

MID-RANGE
Imola Udvarház, Dózsa György tér 4, 3300 Eger, tel: 36 516 180. Superb cuisine in the courtyard of a modern aparthotel by the castle entrance. Recommended: grilled *fogas* followed by date pancake in strawberry sauce – washed down with a 1997 bottle of *Egri Bikavér*.

Pannonia, Kossuth Lajos utca 2, 3530 Miskolc, tel: 46 329 811. The hotel's restaurant has a strong local following; the terrace makes a pleasant summer venue.
Szillagyi, Rákóczi út 5, 3910 Tokaj, tel: 47 352 344. The restaurant of the Tokaj Hotel, near the Tisza Bridge over the Bodrog River, has a charming river terrace for al fresco dining.
Vár Étterem, Kossuth út 93, 3176 Hollókő, tel: 32 379 029. Dine beneath apple and pear trees in the stony courtyard of the UNESCO village restaurant. The Hollókő platter for two at Fts 3,000 is a bargain.

In Eger, **Egertourist**, at Bajcsy-Zsilinsky utca 9 (tel: 36 411 724), includes Eger sightseeing, pleasant trips into Bükk National Park and horse-drawn carriage excursions in Szilvásvárad.
In Miskolc, **Borsod Tourist**, at Széchenyi István utca 35 (tel: 46 350 666), offers sightseeing tours to Eger, trips to Tokaj and the Zemplén Hills and into Bükk National Park.

For further information on Northern Hungary, contact Tourinform offices at Eger (Dobó tér 2, 3300 Eger, tel: 36 321 807) and Miskolc (Mindszent tér 1, 3530 Miskolc, tel: 46 348 921).

Travel Tips

Tourist Information

The **Hungarian National Tourist Office** is represented abroad in the UK (London), the USA (New York), Japan (Tokyo) and throughout Europe. The UK address is 46 Eaton Place, London SW1X 8AL, tel: 020 7823 1032, fax: 020 7823 1459, e-mail: htlondon@hungarytourism.hu In Hungary, **Tourinform Customer Service** – jointly run by the Hungarian National Tourist Office and the Economic Ministry – is at Sütő utca 2, 1052 Budapest, tel: 1 317 9800, fax: 1 317 9656. It provides tourist information in English, Hungarian, German, French, Italian and Russian (open Monday–Friday 09:00–19:00, Saturday, Sunday and holidays 09:00–16:00).
There are Tourinform offices throughout the country (see At a Glance). Others in Budapest are at: Nyugati (Western) Railway Station, Main Hall by platform 10, tel: 1 302 8580 (open 07:00–20:00); VII Király utca 93, tel: 1 352 1433 (open 08:00–20:00); and Castle Hill, I Tárnok utca 9–11, tel: 1 488 0453 (open 08:00–20:00).

Embassies and Consulates

American Embassy, Szabadság tér 12, tel: 1 267 4400 (Pest V). Australian Embassy, Királyhágó tér 8–9, tel: 1 201 8899 (Buda XII). British Embassy, Harmincad utca 6, tel: 1 266 2888 (Pest V). Canadian Embassy, Budakeszi út 32, tel: 1 275 1200 (Buda XII). Irish Embassy, Szabadság tér 7, tel: 1 302 9600 (Pest V). South African Embassy, Gárdonyi Géza út 17, tel: 1 392 0999 (Buda II).

Entry Requirements

Nationals of most European countries, including the UK, and the USA, Canada and South Africa need only a valid passport to stay for up to 90 days. Citizens of Australia, New Zealand and some Asian countries will need a visa.

Customs

The duty-free allowance for goods imported into Hungary is 250 cigarettes (or 50 cigars or 250g of tobacco), a litre of spirits and two litres of wine, plus 250ml of eau de cologne and 100ml of perfume.

Health Requirements

No vaccinations are required to enter Hungary. Free or reduced-cost emergency health treatment is available to British, Scandinavian and most east European visitors. However, all visitors are advised to arrange their own comprehensive travel and medical insurance. Keep receipts and invoices – they will be needed if you make a claim. For emergency telephone numbers, see Health Services on Page 126.

Getting to Hungary

By air: All international flights to Hungary land at Budapest's Ferihegy Airport. Malév Hungarian Airlines and British Airways operate at least one flight daily from London Heathrow; Malév also flies from London Gatwick and Manchester. You can reach Hungary by air from most major European cities, while Malév also flies direct from New York and Toronto. From the airport, a taxi, airport minibus (tel: 296 8555/8993/6283) or Airport Centrum Shuttle Bus will get you to the city centre. Or you can use public transport – the bus with the red 93 number (the black 93 is slower), changing to the blue metro line at the Kőbánya-Kispest terminus.

By road: Hungary is developing a motorway network with Budapest at its hub. The M1 motorway enters the country from Vienna, linking with the M0 ring road around Budapest, the M7 from Lake Balaton, M5 from the south and M3 from the east of the country.

To drive in Hungary, or to hire a car, you need a valid national driving licence; you must also be able to show your car registration document and have a country sticker. Avoid drinking *any* alcohol before driving – even the smallest amount of alcohol in the bloodstream is enough to get you convicted. Use dimmed headlights outside built-up areas, even during daylight hours. Seat belts must be worn in the front of the car (and in the back outside built-up areas); children under 12 are not allowed to travel in the front seats. Driving in Hungary, like the rest of continental Europe, is on the right.

By rail: You can easily reach Hungary by international train from the capitals of neighbouring countries – Vienna (Austria) is 3 hours away, Prague (Czech Republic) 7½ hours and Bratislava (Slovakia) 2 hours 40 minutes. Most international trains arrive in Budapest at the Keleti (Eastern) station.

By bus: Long-distance buses operate to Hungary from the rest of Europe. Eurolines operates a thrice-weekly year-round service from London via Vienna to Győr and Budapest, increasing to five times a week in high summer. Hungarian bus company Volánbusz operates services from a total of 17 European countries; they arrive in Budapest at Volánbusz coach station in Erzsébet tér.

By river: A hydrofoil service operates daily from early spring to late autumn (twice daily from late July to early September) on the Danube from Vienna to Budapest via Bratislava. The 282km (175-mile) Vienna-Budapest journey takes 5½ hours. There is a Danube ferry crossing to Esztergom from Štúrovo in Slovakia.

What to Pack

Remember that Hungary experiences a continental climate, with hot summers and cold winters. From June to September you need only light clothing – take beachwear if you intend spending time stretched out in the sun by Lake Balaton. In late spring and autumn, a fold-up umbrella will deal with the odd shower; pack warmer clothes for the evenings, when the air cools appreciably. In winter go prepared for severe chill, though in equal proportions you may enjoy crisp sunny days or suffer damp and cloudy conditions.

Money Matters

Currency: The unit of currency in Hungary is the forint (abbreviated Ft), divided into 100 fillér. Banknotes are 200, 500, 1000, 2000, 5000 and 10,000 forints; coins are 1, 2, 5, 10, 20, 50 and 100 forints (fillér coins are virtually worthless and are no longer minted). Note that some hotels price their rates in Euros, owing to the changing value of the forint.

Currency exchange: Money and travellers' cheques can be exchanged at banks, exchange bureaux and hotels, though banks offer the best rate. Automatic teller machines (ATMs) are found throughout the country and are by far the easiest way to top up your cash reserves. Forget the street-corner black market – it's illegal, there's little advantage to be gained and you may well be ripped off. If you have forints left over at the end of your visit they can be reconverted, but you will need to produce the original exchange receipt.

Credit cards: The leading credit cards – Visa, American Express and MasterCard – are accepted at most hotels, restaurants, shops and petrol stations. But carry cash as well and be prepared to use it in museums, galleries and supermarkets and for bus and train travel.

Tipping: The custom in Hungarian restaurants is to round up the bill or to add 10 per cent; in a few cases, the bill will include a 10 per cent service charge. Give the tip when the bill arrives and tell the waiter how much, rather than leave the coins on the table. Taxi drivers, hairdressers, beauticians and petrol station attendants are also tipped as a matter of routine.

Taxes: Sales tax (ÁFA) of between 12 and 25 per cent is usually included in the cost of a purchase, but check before you buy. For purchases of 25,000 forints or more, you can claim back the tax before leaving the country. For further advice, contact Europe Tax Free Shopping Hungary at Bég utca 3–5 (Buda II), tel: 1 212 4734.

Accommodation

Visitors to Hungary will find all levels of accommodation, from basic youth hostels and rooms in private homes to full-service five-star hotels. Cities and towns have well-priced mid-range hotels suitable for touring visitors; if you're in Budapest with money to spare you might splash out on a deluxe night or two. In rural areas, there are pensions and inns offering simple accommodation. Tourinform offices can provide information on where to stay in their locality. For advance reservations and advice in the UK, contact Danube Travel, at 45 Great Cumberland Place, London W1H 7LH, tel: 020 7724 7577, fax: 020 7224 8959.

Eating Out

Hungary prides itself on its cuisine, and with good reason. You will never have trouble finding somewhere warm and inviting to eat – and with prices extremely affordable by western European standards, you might find yourself not even bothering to look at the price before ordering. In Budapest, you can seek out every kind of ethnic eatery – from Mexican to Mongolian, Greek to Korean. Restaurants serving traditional Hungarian fare can be found in abundance throughout the country, with a range of Hungary's fine quality wines to accompany your meal.

Transport

Hungary's rail network radiates from Budapest, with trains departing from one of three termini – Keleti, the eastern station; Nyugati, the western station; and Déli, across the river in Buda. Points served from Keleti include Békéscsaba, Eger, Győr, Keszthely, Lake Balaton, Miskolc, Sopron, Szolnok and Szombathely; from Nyugati, trains run to Debrecen, Kecskemét, Szeged and Záhony; from Déli there are departures for Kaposvár and Pécs. There are seven-day and 10-day rail passes for tourists and a Lake Balaton day ticket giving unlimited travel around the lake. Information on domestic rail services is available on 1 461 5400 (24 hours). Hungary also boasts 16 narrow-gauge railways, scattered throughout the country and operating along a total 380km (236 miles) of track.

Steam-hauled 'nostalgia' trains run from Keszthely to Badacsony and from Budapest's Nyugati station to Szob on the Danube Bend in summer. For information, tel: 1 318 1704.

Within Budapest, the three underground railway lines of the Metro converge at Deák tér, on the Pest side of the river. Trains run at intervals of up to 12 minutes – every two minutes in the rush-hour – from 04:30 until 23:10. The HÉV suburban railway has four lines, three on the Pest side of the city and the fourth serving Óbuda, Aquincum and Szentendre on the Danube Bend.

Buses: Volánbusz, the national Hungarian bus

CONVERSION CHART		
FROM	**TO**	**MULTIPLY BY**
Millimetres	Inches	0.0394
Metres	Yards	1.0936
Metres	Feet	3.281
Kilometres	Miles	0.6214
Square kilometres	Square miles	0.386
Hectares	Acres	2.471
Litres	Pints	1.760
Kilograms	Pounds	2.205
Tonnes	Tons	0.984
To convert Celsius to Fahrenheit: x 9 ÷ 5 + 32		

operator, runs 108 services throughout the country, many of them radiating from Budapest's two coach hubs – Erzsébet tér bus station and the Népstadion bus station. For information on bus services within Hungary, tel: 1 317 2966 (Erzsébet tér bus station); 1 252 4498 (Népstadion bus station); or 1 329 1450 (Árpád híd bus station, for Danube Bend).

In Budapest, trams and buses offer a comprehensive service around the city. Trolleybuses run mainly to the north and east of downtown Pest. Buses run every 10–20 minutes from 05:00 until 23:00 throughout the city and are useful in Buda's hilly areas. Night buses operate on 17 routes and carry an 'É' suffix.

Road: Hungary has five motorways, three of which – the M3 from Budapest to Füzesabony via Gyöngyös; M5 from Budapest to Kecskemét and Kiskunfélegyháza; and part of the M1, between Győr and Hegyeshalom – require a toll to be paid. The roads are generally good, well sign-posted and relatively free of traffic; in northern Hungary and on the Great Plain you could drive for miles without seeing another vehicle.

The speed limit for cars is 120 km/h (70 mph) on motorways, 100 km/h (60 mph) on dual carriageways, 80 km/h (50 mph) on single carriageways and 50 km/h (30 mph) in built-up areas.

Car rental: The leading international car-rental companies are represented in Hungary,

along with local firms. Companies include Avis, Budget and Hertz, all with rental desks at Budapest's Ferihegy airport.

Business Hours

Banks are open from 08:00 until 14:00 Monday to Thursday, occasionally later, and 08:00 until 13:00 on Friday; they are closed on Saturday and Sunday. In Budapest, some *bureaux de change* are open at weekends. Principal post offices open from 08:00 until 18:00 or 19:00 Monday to Friday and until 13:00 on Saturday; minor post offices close at 15:30 and don't open at weekends. Shopping hours roughly correspond to those of other central European towns and cities. Most supermarkets are open from 09:00 until 19:00 from Monday to Friday; 07:00 until 13:00 on Saturday with some opening on Sundays. The word 'nonstop' translates as being open 24 hours, whether convenience grocery store or all-night café. Other shops and department stores tend to open from 10:00 until 18:00 Monday to Friday and 09:00 until 13:00 on Saturday. Some department stores keep longer hours and in Budapest, large shopping centres like the Westend Centre remain open until 02:00 at weekends.

Museums are generally open from 10:00 until 18:00 from Tuesday to Sunday between April and October (10:00 until 16:00 in winter). They are closed on Monday.

USEFUL PHRASES	
How are you?	• *Hogy van?*
Do you speak English?	• *Beszél angolul?*
I don't speak Hungarian	• *Nem tudok magyarul*
What is your name?	• *Mi a neve?*
My name is …	• *A nevem …*
How much is this?	• *Mennyibe kerül?*
I would like …	• *Kérek szépen …*
The bill, please	• *Kérem a számlát*
What is the time?	• *Hány óra?*
Good day	• *Jó napot*
Good morning	• *Jó reggelt*
Good evening	• *Jó estét*
Goodnight	• *Jó éjszakát*
Goodbye	• *Viszlát*
Yes/No	• *Igen/Nem*
Please/thank you	• *Kérem/Köszönöm*
Sorry	• *Bocsánat*
Left/Right	• *Bal/Jobb*
airport	• *repülőtér*
alley	• *fasor, köz*
arrival	• *érkezés*
avenue	• *út, útja*
boat	• *hajó*
boulevard	• *körút*
bridge	• *híd*
bus	• *busz*
cafe	• *kávéház*
circle	• *körönd*
closed	• *zárva*
departure	• *indulás*
embankment	• *rakpart*
entrance	• *bejárat*
exit	• *kijárat*
highway	• *autópálya*
hill	• *hegy*
island	• *sziget*
ladies' room	• *nők, hölgyek*
men's room	• *férfiak, urak*
open	• *nyitva*
platform	• *peron*
prohibited	• *tilos*
restaurant	• *étterem*
square	• *tér, tere*
station	• *állomás*
street	• *utca*
train	• *vonat*

Time Difference

Hungary is on Central European Time, one hour ahead of GMT in winter and two hours ahead of GMT in summer (the last Sunday in March until the last Sunday in October). The 24-hour clock is widely used.

Communications

International telephone calls can be made from public call boxes – dial 00, wait for the dialling tone and then dial the country code, area code and number required. Public phone boxes with a red target and black-and-white arrow on the door display a call-back number, which you can give to the person you are calling – the dialling code for Hungary is 0036. Phone numbers in Budapest are seven-digit (area code 1); others have eight digits, including the two-digit area code. Phone cards of 50 and 120 units can be bought in post offices, newsagents or from tobacconists.

Electricity

In Hungary the power supply is 220 volts, 50 cycles. Sockets are two-pin and an adaptor is needed for British, American and Australian appliances.

Weights and Measures

Hungary uses the metric system for all measurements (*see* the conversion table on page 124).

Health Services

American Clinic, Hattyú utca 14, Budapest I, tel: 224 9090 (24-hour emergency service). Falck SOS Hungary, Kapy utca 49, Budapest II, tel: 200 0100 (24-hour outpatient service). Dental emergencies (24 hours) in Budapest, tel: 317 6600, 267 9602 and 342 2546. Pharmacies (24 hours) in Budapest, tel: 314 3694 and 355 4727.

Personal Safety

Hungary is no less safe than the majority of other European countries and there is little risk to tourists. But visitors should be on their guard against petty theft – entrust your valuables to a hotel safe rather than carry-ing them with you and beware of pickpockets. In Budapest, it's wise to steer clear of the area between Rákóczi tér, the red light district, and the Keleti railway terminus.

Emergencies

Ambulance, tel: 104 (in English, 1 111 1666).
Police, tel: 107.
Fire, tel: 105.
Motoring assistance, tel: 1 155 0379.
Other useful numbers:
Directory enquiries, tel: 198 (domestic), 199 (international). Hungarian Disabled Association (MEOSZ), tel: 1 388 8951 (08:00–16:00 weekdays).

Language

Hungarian is a difficult language to learn, so any attempt to speak it is well received. Even *köszönöm* (thank you) in appreciation of services rendered is better than nothing. In Budapest, you will get by with German, while English may be under-stood in hotels and restaurants, but in provincial Hungary the vast majority of people speak only Hungarian.

GOOD READING

Tökés, Rudolf (1996) *Hungary's Negotiated Revolution,* Cambridge University Press.
Gerő, András and Pető, Iván (1999) *Unfinished Socialism,* Central European University Press.
Lukács, John (1989) *Budapest 1900,* Weidenfeld.
Hoensch, Jörg (1988) *A History of Modern Hungary,* Longman.
Leigh Fermor, Patrick (1988) *Between the Woods and the Water,* Penguin.
Pressburger, Giorgio and Nicola (1990) *Homage to the Eighth District,* Readers International.
Lang, George (1992) *The Cuisine of Hungary,* Corvina.
Hofer, Tamás (1975) *Hungarian Folk Art,* Corvina.

INDEX

Note: Numbers in **bold**
indicate photographs